COOKING WITH MS. LARTHY
Life Lessons in Soul and Soul Food
by
Tom Graves with Larthy Washington

Devault Graves Books, Memphis

DEVAULT GRAVES BOOKS

Cooking With Ms. Larthy is copyright © 2020 by Tom Graves and Larthy Washington. Published by Devault Graves Books, Memphis, Tennessee. All rights reserved. This book, or parts thereof, may not be reproduced in any form, except for the inclusion of brief quotations in a review, without the permission of the publisher.

Print book ISBN: 978-1-942531-38-8

eBook ISBN: 978-1-942531-39-5

Cover design and layout: Patrick Alley

Cover photo: Susan Van Dyck

On my day off, I rarely want to eat restaurant food . . . what I want to eat is home cooking, somebody's **anybody's** *– mother's or grandmother's food.*
— *Anthony Bourdain*

. . . no one is born a great cook, one learns by doing.
— *Julia Child*

Chefs are not generally the best source for recipes. They don't use them the way we do at home.
—*Sam Sifton,*
The New York Times

TABLE OF CONTENTS

Introduction
A Note on the Cooking and the Recipes
The Nine-Year-Old Cook
Ms. Larthy's Cooking Tips

Recipes

Main Attractions (Meat and Poultry)
- Sunday Dinner Fried Chicken
- Baked Chicken
- Fried Pork Chops
- Smothered Pork Chops
- Ms. Larthy's Oven-Baked Pork Chops
- Turkey Necks
- Pork Neckbones
- Oxtails
- The Gay Hawk Restaurant's Peppery Ham Shanks
- Beer Can Chicken
- Ms. Larthy's Oven Bar-b-q Chicken
- Ms. Larthy's Oven Bar-b-q Pulled Pork
- Ms. Larthy's Twice-Baked Meatloaf
- Lovin' in the Oven BBQ Pork Loin
- The Great American Hamburger
- Dana's Cheddar Wings
- Let's Cheat A Bit Chicken and Dumplings
- Ms. Larthy's Chicken Salad
- Fried Steak and Gravy

Does It Swim? (Fish and Seafood)
- Pan-Fried Catfish Fillets
- BBQ Shrimp

Soups, Stews, Gumbos, Etc.
- An Authentic Cajun Roux
- Roux Microwave Shortcut
- Tom's Real Kitchen Shrimp and Sausage Gumbo
- Chicken and Andouille Sausage Gumbo
- Bintou's African Chicken Stew

Chili Cook-Off
Pressure Cooker Split Pea Soup
Ms. Larthy's Leftover Beef Roast Stew

Eat Your Vegetables
Tom's White Beans and Rice
Ms. Larthy's Extra Tasty Green Beans
Black-Eyed Peas
Soul-Style Boiled Cabbage
Home Fries
White Potatoes With Cheese
El Perfecto Baked Potato
Skillet-Fried Corn
Ms. Larthy's Fried Corn on the Cob
Smothered Broccoli
Ooh Boy Broccoli Salad
Not Too Slimy Boiled Okra
Hollerin' For Them Collards (Collard Greens)
Fried Okra
Fried Green Tomatoes

Breads
Cornbreads Three
    Ms. Larthy's Good & Grainy Cornbread Muffins
    Mom's Index Card Cornbread
    "Jiffy" Mix Cornbread
My Best (So Far) Buttermilk Biscuit Recipe
Ms. Peggy's Big Batch O' Biscuits
Mom's Quick Homemade Rolls

Sweet Tooth (Desserts)
Ms. Larthy's Chocolate Pound Cake
Your Basic Chocolate Cake
7-Up Cake
My Granny's "Pink Lady" Strawberry Cake
Not From Scratch But So What? Strawberry Cake
Fresh Apple Cake
Ms. Larthy's Classic Karo Pecan Pie
My Mom's Pecan Pie Varation
Yvonne Mitchell's Bourbon Pecan Pie
Old Fashioned Apple Pie
Lemon Ice Box Pie

Ms. Larthy's Fried Peach Pie
Ms. Larthy's Old Fashioned Peach Cobbler
Sweet Potato Pie
Ms. Larthy's Better Than Scratch Banana Pudding
Mom's Peanut Butter Cookies
Mom's Lady Fingers

Whistle Wetters (Beverages)

Aunt Merle's Secret Sweet Tea
Ms. Larthy's Special Party Tea
Traditional Ethiopian Hot Tea With Milk
Punch It Up Fruit Punch
Don't Fail Me Fruit Smoothie
Authentic African Ginger Beer
The Ernest Hemingway Original El Floridita Daiquiri
Singapore Sling

Side Attractions

Ms. Larthy's Work of Art Macaroni and Cheese
Ethan's Mac and Cheese
Ms. Larthy's Handmade Spaghetti and Meatballs
Ms. Larthy's Lasagna
The Only Good Homemade Pizza
Ms. Larthy's Broccoli Alfredo with Hickory Smoked Sausage
Ms. Larthy's Sunday School Social Potato Salad
The American Grilled Cheese Sandwich
Baked Bean Super Side Dish
Cole Slaw
Mo Carlson's Fandibulous Tomato Dressing
Mom's Shish-Kabob Marinade
Tom Graves' Exquisite Bay Leaf Barbecue Table Sauce
The Simple Truth Barbecue Basting Sauce
Final Touch Barbecue Sauce
DIY BBQ Rub
Aunt Nora's Buttered and Roasted Pecans
Fresh Pineapple and Curry Powder

Christmas Dinner

Cornbread Dressing
Coconut Pineapple Cake
Turnip Greens

WHO DID WHAT? (WHO CREATED THOSE RECIPES?)

Recipes created by Ms. Larthy Washington

Sunday Dinner Fried Chicken
Baked Chicken
Fried Pork Chops
Ms. Larthy's Oven-Baked Pork Chops
Pork Neckbones
Ms. Larthy's Oven Bar-b-q Chicken
Ms. Larthy's Oven Bar-b-q Pulled Pork
Ms. Larthy's Twice-Baked Meatloaf
Lovin' in the Oven BBQ Pork Loin
Let's Cheat A Bit Chicken and Dumplings
Ms. Larthy's Chicken Salad
Fried Steak and Gravy
Pan-Fried Catfish Fillets
Ms. Larthy's Soul Chili
Ms. Larthy's Leftover Beef Stew
Ms. Larthy's Extra Tasty Green Beans
Black-Eyed Peas
Soul-Style Boiled Cabbage
Home Fries
White Potatoes With Cheese
Skillet-Fried Corn
Ms. Larthy's Fried Corn on the Cob
Smothered Broccoli
Ooh Boy Broccoli Salad
Not Too Slimy Boiled Okra
Hollerin' For Them Collards (Collard Greens)
Fried Okra
Fried Green Tomatoes
Ms. Larthy's Good & Grainy Cornbread Muffins
Ms. Larthy's Chocolate Pound Cake
Your Basic Chocolate Cake
7-Up Cake
Not From Scratch But So What? Strawberry Cake
Fresh Apple Cake
Ms. Larthy's Classic Karo Pecan Pie
Old Fashioned Apple Pie

Lemon Ice Box Pie
Ms. Larthy's Fried Peach Pie
Ms. Larthy's Old Fashioned Peach Cobbler
Sweet Potato Pie
Ms. Larthy's Better Than Scratch Banana Pudding
Ms. Larthy's Special Party Tea
Punch It Up Fruit Punch
Ms. Larthy's Work of Art Macaroni and Cheese
Ms. Larthy's Handmade Spaghetti and Meatballs
Ms. Larthy's Lasagna
Ms. Larthy's Broccoli Alfredo with Hickory Smoked Sausage
Ms. Larthy's Sunday School Social Potato Salad
Baked Bean Super Side Dish
Cole Slaw
Cornbread Dressing
Coconut Pineapple Cake
Turnip Greens

Recipes created by Tom Graves

Smothered Pork Chops
Beer Can Chicken
The Great American Hamburger
BBQ Shrimp
An Authentic Cajun Roux
Roux Microwave Shortcut
Tom's Real Kitchen Shrimp and Sausage Gumbo
Chicken and Andouille Sausage Gumbo
Tom's True Blue Texas Chili
Pressure Cooker Split Pea Soup
Tom's White Beans and Rice
El Perfecto Baked Potato
My Best (So Far) Buttermilk Biscuit Recipe
Traditional Ethiopian Hot Tea With Milk
Don't Fail Me Now Fruit Smoothie
The Ernest Hemingway Original El Floridita Daiquiri
Singapore Sling
The American Grilled Cheese Sandwich
Tom Graves' Exquisite Bay Leaf Barbecue Table Sauce
The Simple Truth Barbecue Basting Sauce

Final Touch Barbecue Sauce
DIY BBQ Rub
Fresh Pineapple and Curry Powder

Recipes created by Emma Sue Graves-Elkins (My Mom)

My Mom's Pecan Pie Variation
Mom's Peanut Butter Cookies
Mom's Lady Fingers
Mom's Shish-Kabob Marinade
Mom's Index Card Cornbread

Recipes created by Other Folks

Turkey Necks – Dana Merriweather
Oxtails – Eliza Jubert
The Gay Hawk Restaurant's Peppery Ham Shanks – Terica Bobo and Georgia Noel
Dana's Cheddar Wings – Dana Merriweather
Bintou's African Chicken Stew – Bintou Ndiaye
Di's Kickin' Chili – Lydia Dianne Lay
Ms. Peggy's Big Batch O' Biscuits – Peggy Brown
My Granny's Strawberry Cake – Jasmine Parks
Yvonne Mitchell's Bourbon Pecan Pie – Yvonne Mitchell
Aunt Merle's Secret Sweet Tea – Merle Graves
Authentic African Ginger Beer – Bintou Ndiaye
Ethan's Mac and Cheese – Yvonne Mitchell
The Only Good Homemade Pizza – James Newcomb
Mo Carlson's Fandibulous Tomato Dressing – Mo Carlson
Aunt Nora's Buttered and Roasted Pecans – Nora MacAlexander

INTRODUCTION

This book was born of frustration. During the summer of 2016 I had ruined my third batch of fried catfish, a dish we Southerners crave. Three times over that summer I had rendered it inedible. Spitting a mouthful of catfish out onto my plate, cursing that I'd have to go out somewhere and find something decent to eat yet again, a little oddball thought danced its way into my mind: I sure wish some older black lady would teach me how to cook soul food. From A to Z.

No one had ever taught me to cook. What I knew I had learned completely from books. I have a kitchen cabinet full of cookbooks. But I have no native knowledge at all about how to prepare the comfort food I most love. Soul food and country cooking are two sides of the same Southern coin. And they are euphemisms. Soul food means black cooking and country means white cooking. Are there differences? A few. But the similarities are so much more.

My mother at the time of this writing is 87 years old and still of reasonable body and mind, although greatly slowed down by her advancing years.[1] She does not cook any longer and has not in several years. May she forgive me should she ever read this, but my mom was never much of a cook, unlike my grandmother, who cooked fantastically. Oh, relatives always bragged that my mom was just terrific in the kitchen, but as someone who sat at her table three times a day for 22 years I'm here to tell you that wasn't so. My whole early life I would barely eat her cooking and I had a beanpole silhouette because of it. I especially could not eat her vegetables. They tasted like cardboard. On a good day. In high school I read the unforgettable short story "The Patented Gate and the Mean Hamburger" by fellow Southerner Robert Penn Warren and came across a passage that explained it all to me. In the story Warren reveals why poor country folk were so mad for hamburgers:

"But all those folks, like Jeff York and his family, like hamburgers, with pickle and onions and mustard and tomato catsup, the whole works. It is something different. They stay out in the country and eat hog meat, when they can get it, and greens and corn bread and potatoes, and nothing but a pinch of salt to brighten it on the tongue, and when they get to town and get hold of beef and wheat bread and all the stuff to jack up the flavor, they have to swallow to keep the mouth from flooding before they even take the first bite."

There it was, "nothing but a pinch of salt to brighten it on the tongue." That was my mom. No flavor. No seasoning. In my mother's defense, I have to say she made excellent desserts, and I have included some of her best recipes in this book. Mom, like me, had a sweet tooth, and satisfied it with cakes and pies and pastries and something new and creative all the time. Mom became so good at baking cakes and decorating them that her wedding cakes and birthday cakes were in great demand in our Parkway Village neighborhood in Memphis and she turned her talents into a small cottage business, enough to keep her in some folding money. Enough that my brother, Norris, and I can barely stand to eat cake to this day and will not touch icing.

[1] My mother, Emma Sue Graves-Elkins, passed away just as I began writing this book.

But my mom's skinny and eldest boy (me) started to grow up and though still living at home with the parents went off to college every weekday at Memphis State University, meeting new people, exploring new worlds, and for the first time eating exotic foods that he wouldn't have touched with ten-foot tongs only a few years earlier. And he, me, couldn't ever get enough. I had discovered food. That skinny boy began to muscle up and by graduation was beginning to look more like a football player than the basketball player I was always mistaken for.

After graduation from Memphis State I wasted no time in getting married to a nice Italian girl who could cook, but hated to, and thus began the long cycle of eating out. We raised a lovely daughter, Allison, who ate reasonably well, and after 23 years my wife and I decided to go our separate ways, as so many do. Single again, I painted the town every color of the rainbow for several years and then went completely mad and married a beautiful and charming West African from Senegal. Bintou Ndiaye was a terrific cook and when homesick for her native cuisine would prepare wonderfully exotic dishes—cassava leaf anyone?—which I very much enjoyed. But she hated cooking just as much as my first wife, yet never tired of *my* cooking. In fact, even though as I write this she and I have been divorced now for over eight years, she still comes over periodically to eat my gumbo and other Cajun dishes.

At present, I am between wives, an aging bachelor with an undiminished appetite and no one to cook for me. Thus three batches of ruined catfish. And the germ of an idea for a way to improve my culinary circumstances and write a book about the experience.

A NOTE ON THE COOKING AND THE RECIPES

Shortly after I first got married, I found myself idle one day while my wife, Denise, was at work at a local hospital where she was a heart echocardiography technician. I knew next to nothing about cooking at that time in my life, but that sure didn't stop me, and I had sent off for a chili recipe booklet from, of all places, the Marlboro cigarette company. One particular recipe intrigued me, one that called for several cloves of minced garlic. I went to the nearby market, rounded up all the ingredients, and brought them back home to make a surprise dinner for the little lady.

I did not know the difference between a head of garlic and a clove of garlic. I tried to mince one of the garlic heads by hand and found that the task was far beyond my kitchen skills. Clever lad that I am, however, I decided the Waring blender that had been a wedding gift would do a fine job of grinding up those tough garlic thingamabobs. So, I inserted them into the blender, pressed the button, and presto!, a minute later I had finely minced garlic.

Undaunted, I stirred the garlic into the chili fixings in a pot with a nice flame underneath, sending a sickeningly pungent odor into every square inch of the house and out into the front and backyards. Still wondering if I had made a wrong turn somewhere, the wife arrived and nearly retched as she walked into the kitchen. I explained what I was doing and she instantly seized on my mistake, in language that began to blister the paint and wilt the houseplants.

That batch of chili went straight into the garbage can, was then taken out to the bigger garbage can out by the curb, carted off by the sanitation trucks, and today is still radiating stink waves in a landfill somewhere, making a no-fly zone for vampires in the Memphis area. Sometimes I think I still smell that garlic.

And now 40 years later I have someone to finally teach me the basics of good cooking.

When I began this project I was adamant that I did not want someone to partner up with who had worked in a restaurant or in any professional cooking capacity. The reason is because chefs and professional cooks do not prepare food for the family table. They prepare food for masses of people, many of whom are highly discriminating gourmands who place a variety of demands on those who prepare their food. Chefs prepare elaborate, highly-seasoned foods using ingredients and methods not typically found in most households. They use industrial kitchen tools and appliances that can do things ordinary homes cannot. One reason homemade pizzas are seldom the equal of those from your favorite pizzeria is because your oven can't remotely compete with the high heat of the professional ones.

Home cooking is what I was after and I wanted someone whose reputation as a cook, someone who had mastered soul food cuisine, was unimpeachable. I wanted someone who had *real* recipes, home recipes, perfected in a real kitchen, in a real home, and prepared for the family dinner. Something that I could learn and duplicate myself, something readers of this book could also duplicate with confidence right in their own kitchens. I knew such a person was bound to be found in my hometown of Memphis, where soul food is everywhere. I thought I would need an audition process and I came up with a list of questions for the applicants, preparing myself to interview at least a dozen people.

And then Larthy Washington walked in the door of the meeting room.

The first person I thought to call to help me find the right partner for this book was Reverend Roger Brown, the pastor of The Greater White Stone Missionary Baptist Church. Reverend Brown also worked as a fund-raiser for LeMoyne-Owen College, where I was a professor of English until my retirement in 2019. I always enjoyed being around Roger Brown, buoyed by his friendliness and sense of humor, and was well aware that he had connections everywhere in Memphis. I just *knew* he'd know someone who fit the idea of what I needed. When I called him and told him I wanted an older lady to teach me how to cook soul food for a book, he was saying "Larthy Washington" before I could finish my sentence. He arranged for me to meet her and as soon as I laid eyes on her I got that weird ESP vibe I've had my entire life as a writer—an internal hum, a tuning fork, that says "Yes, Yes, YES!!! She's the one! Don't blow it!"

The interview became, really, an extended, warm conversation. Ms. Larthy, as I elected to call her with her and her family's permission—my Southern upbringing does not allow me to call anyone older than myself by their first name—had cooked for her family since she was a little girl (more about that later) and those talents flowered in later life when she cooked for her children and husband and then for events at her church, Greater White Stone Missionary Baptist, where she had been a devoted member since 1961. Her cooking at her church took on a life of its own; she was in constant demand for all manner of church functions and gatherings. She learned how to prepare food in the church kitchen for small groups as well as large gatherings. Her cooking was appreciated enough that the church got a couple of plaques to hang outside the kitchen letting everyone know this was "Larthy's Kitchen." To see her in action in this kitchen is to know absolutely it is Larthy's Kitchen. At the age of 80, with arthritis twisting some of her fingers just as it has knotted a few of mine, she is as graceful as a Bolshoi dancer, totally comfortable in her element, with seldom a wasted motion, a quiet confidence borne of thousands of hours spent near a stove, a patience and calm when adjustments to her cooking must be made.

Tom Graves

Tom Graves

    This book contains recipes that Ms. Larthy and I worked on together in the Greater Stone kitchen, her teaching me step-by-step, teaspoon-by-measuring cup. Eighty percent of the recipes in this book are hers, made from scratch in the church kitchen, with me jotting down and confirming every step along the way. And getting to eat afterwards, a great reward I must tell you. When Ms. Larthy uses a brand name product, I name it. For example, she uses Aunt Jemima brand cornmeal in her cornbread muffin recipes. She uses Mango Tang in her wonderful tea. Using items from the grocery store shelf rather than spending needless hours creating ingredients from scratch is a necessary fact of life for today's workers who have limited time to fuss over recipes in their kitchens.

    Because this book is about a sharing of lives—Ms. Larthy's and mine—and the coming together of black and white peoples in our hometown, I share some of my recipes as well. Some recipes are ones I've developed over time, such as my gumbo recipe. In spite of my fumbles and failures in the kitchen over these many years,

I've still managed to get a few things right. I also share a few of my favorite recipes from family and friends and an ex-wife or two, all of whom are properly credited here. *My mother passed away just as I began work with Ms. Larthy for this book. Mom was very interested in the idea and she and I took down a box of her favorite old recipes and began to go through them. I have added some of her best dishes, each one something that easily fits into the broad definition of soul food cooking.,

Soul food is another way of saying that these are recipes from a folk tradition. A tradition very much, as I see it, in danger of being lost to future generations. Many young people today elect not to cook at all, or cook faddish dishes that were not part of their parents' generational cuisine. I mean, who ever heard of arugula 50 years ago?

Another problem for me is what is offered in many soul food cookbooks, including those that are award-winning and highly lauded. Edna Lewis and her best-selling cookbooks may be the best-known of dozens, if not hundreds, of soul food titles. My problem with most of these books is that they try ferociously to elevate a humble, everyday cuisine into something much more haute and to my taste much more haughty. Just look at the long lists of hard-to-get ingredients. Look at the sometimes days of preparation required for even simple dishes. These recipes, my friends, are made not for you and me, but to impress other chefs. To win awards. To get the attention of the James Beard people. Then there are the other books that want to focus on the most backwater, arcane, and halfway-demented dishes that can be found in the Deep South, like those unspeakable "vittles" Granny would cook up on *The Beverly Hillbillies*. So, for this book we'll leave out the hog snouts, the skillet-fried chicken feet, possum and yams, potato chip sandwiches, the brains-and-whatever.

As a wannabe cook, nothing angers me as much as a recipe that doesn't work. Because of the high praise it received in *The New York Times*, I bought the republished version of *Princess Pamela's Soul Food Cookbook*. Looking for something to try-out from the book I saw the recipe for stewed chicken wings, which I happened to have on hand in the freezer. I prepared the recipe precisely as written and the result was a tasteless muck. It was a big-time recipe fail and someone, somewhere should have caught and corrected this flawed recipe before it went into print for thousands of people to choke on. Just this week I tried a recipe for the rolls that were made for years in Memphis City Schools that was published in the local newspaper. I would save my money up in middle school just to buy those rolls, they were so mouth-watering. The recipe was a complete failure, the dough so watery that it could not be rolled out at all as per instructions. The dough had to be glopped onto the baking sheet like drop biscuits. The result was over-sugared stones.

I pledge and promise that the recipes in this book work. I know because they have all been kitchen tested by Ms. Larthy and yours truly. In a real kitchen, not an industrial kitchen where chefs experiment with their industrial recipes. I should add that if two people cook the same recipe following the instructions carefully and precisely, they are likely to get varying results. Why? Even minute differences in stoves (gas or electric?), ovens, cookware, and even something as basic as how someone stirs, can adversely affect a dish. To perfect a recipe requires patience (which I'm short on) and practice and many times making adjustments to suit your personal tastes or to fine tune based on your kitchen amenities.

I also want to say this: For a number of years in my early career I was the copywriter for Richards Medical Company which evolved into Smith + Nephew, one of the world's leading manufacturers of orthopedic implants. Not only did I write the advertisements for these products that went into medical journals, but I also wrote the surgical techniques and procedures for these products. This required highly-detailed, micro-precise instructions that surgeons could follow to a tee without confusion or failure. Faulty instructions could cost lives, so I had to do a plu-perfect job of writing these techniques and my work was overseen by a phalanx of surgeon consultants, lawyers, and marketing heads. Nothing could be *almost* right. It had to be *exactly* right. I have applied those standards to the book you hold in your hands.

Ms. Larthy and I want you to not only *try* our recipes but to find *love* in our recipes. That is our secret ingredient. One other thing: we have, as a culture in America, gotten very used to highly-flavored processed foods—junk food—that have literally been engineered by flavor engineers—guys in white lab coats—who over a period of decades have so over-stimulated our taste faculties that we often find real kitchen-cooked foods like the ones you find in this book a trifle bland. I'm convinced that the reason Kentucky Fried Chicken became so popular in the early 1960s is because the chicken was so outrageously flavor-bombed that when compared to the average housewife's version no one could resist the fireworks going on when they took a bite of the Colonel's product. When the cost of a frying chicken, oil, flour, seasonings, and other things were taken into account to feed a family of, let's say, four, the Colonel's bucket was just as cheap. Many moms opted out of their kitchen duties when it came to fried chicken, especially when everyone was clamoring for the KFC.

I keep repeating the word "real" with these recipes. They are just that, real, cooked in a real kitchen, by a real soul food cook who isn't jacking-up the flavors for restaurant customers, but teaching a beginner, a learner, *me*, how it's all done. The flavors are going to be more subtle, less overwhelming, and ultimately more satisfying. *Real*. When this book is finished, if nothing else comes of it, I will have learned to cook for myself and to enjoy meals cooked with my own two hands.

And for that I have only Ms. Larthy to thank.

---

*NOTE: The spellings barbecue, bar-b-q, and BBQ are used interchangeably in this book. In Memphis it is impossible to adhere to any one spelling. As long as it tastes good does it really matter?

Tom Graves

Ms. Larthy Washington in her favorite place, the church kitchen.

THE NINE-YEAR-OLD COOK

When Larthy Ree Rogers was nine years old her family felt that she might be old enough to start cooking the midday family meal. Born in 1937 in the depths and desperation of the Great Depression in rural Mississippi, 20 miles from Tupelo, the nearest town of any size, she had been raised in a family of African Americans who all owned and farmed their own properties. Her grandparents on her mother's side, the Hodges, owned 80 acres and had given her parents a plot to work and live on. Her father's folks owned acreage about ten miles away. Although much of Mississippi was still steeped in the legacy of Jim Crow and white supremacy, this part of Northeast Mississippi, far outside the parameters of the Mississippi Delta, seemed to have a calmer attitude about race. A great number of blacks who lived in the region farmed their own land and survived those perilous economic times in relative peace without the horrors and violence that seemed endemic to so much of Mississippi.

Only a year before Larthy was born, nearby Tupelo was nearly blown off the map by one of the worst tornadoes in U.S. history. It leveled 48 city blocks, killing over 200 people and injuring nearly 1,000 more. One survivor of the storm was a baby named Elvis Presley. Larthy's older brother, Harvey, also survived.

"We were poor, but we didn't really know it," says Larthy today, a sentiment often heard from those who grew up during the Depression. Her family was small by Depression standards, just her mother, father, and brother besides herself. Almost from birth she was expected to do chores, which included milking 15 cows twice per day and putting 20 gallons on the road every single morning without fail. When asked if she did any of the milking, Larthy laughs and says, "Oh, sure!"

"Just being one girl and one boy, I did everything my brother did," she says. "If he went to chop wood for Daddy, I was there. We'd strip sorghum to take to the mill to make sorghum molasses, and I was there. When we chopped cotton, I was there. When we picked cotton, I was there. When we pulled peanuts, I was there. We dug potatoes. I was there."

Larthy didn't always care for some of the foods she was surrounded by. "I didn't much like the sorghum," she states. "But my brother would practically drink it. He *loved* it. We would kill the hogs and get streak o' lean meat. Daddy had him a little hut where he would build a fire and smoke it.

"I never could eat the streak o' lean or bacon either for that matter. I guess because I knew where it came from. No, I didn't eat chitlins either. I made sure to go to school on the days Daddy would kill hogs because I was not going to be bothered with them chitlins. By the time I'd get home that day, all that mess with them hogs would be done."

Little Larthy was only eight years old when she began to take an interest in cooking. It was watching her maternal grandmother, Gertrude Hodges, at the kitchen stove when her curiosity began to be piqued. "My grandmother was *the* cook," she says. "She almost never went to the field. She stayed in the house most of the time cooking and doing things. She had also cooked for a white family in town and helped raise their children. Everything I'd see her do in the kitchen, I'd ask her if I could do it too. From when I was a little bitty girl I'd be right on her apron strings. 'Can I do it? Let me do it, Grandma!' And I just went from that."

Right after breakfast the whole family would go to the field to start the day's work, whether it was chopping cotton, picking cotton, or any of a dozen other chores. When Larthy was nine years old, at ten o'clock sharp she was told to go back to the house to start "dinner," the big midday meal not to be confused with supper, which in the rural South consisted of leftovers from the noon-time meal. She did this all by herself, starting a fire in the wood stove and preparing mostly vegetables picked fresh from the family garden. A typical meal might consist of beans and potatoes flavored with pork, sweet potatoes, cornbread, and milk. Butter would also be on the table that had been churned by her mother in a big stone churn. Meat—pork and chicken typically—was saved for weekends, particularly Sundays. Occasionally there would be beef from a cow the family had slaughtered. Also her father and brother hunted rabbits and squirrels, which made for some fine eating. "It wasn't unusual," Larthy says "for Daddy to go off hunting and come back with 15 rabbits. Some folks would eat coon meat, but we wouldn't. Daddy didn't go deer hunting, so we didn't get deer meat either. My uncle died from exposure after deer hunting out in the cold."

When Larthy left the field at ten o'clock every morning her folks could watch her from the nearby field all the way until she was safe inside the house. "When you get there now, don't forget to lock the doors," she remembers her folks saying and then laughs. "That is funny to me because nobody ever locked their doors back then. What we'd do is take a chair and turn it backwards up by the door which would denote that we were gone off somewhere and would soon be back. Nobody would come in once they saw that chair turned backwards.

"I guess I inherited all my cooking from my grandmother. My mother was a good cook, but she was a lazy cook (laughs). She was so glad when I got big enough to cook. I could probably count the meals she cooked after I started cooking."

The simple truth was Larthy loved to cook and was good at it. As she grew up, the kitchen more and more became her special place, her refuge, and it remains so to this day. Hanging in the kitchen at Greater White Stone Baptist Church in Memphis is a plaque that church members bought for her that reads "Larthy's Kitchen."

The Rogers family lived a humble but happy life in this part of rural Mississippi. "Going to town" meant getting a ride to Tupelo, the big city in those parts where a young girl from the country would be dazzled by things like the movies, hamburgers and Coca-Colas, and all manner of enticing goods at the shops along the main streets. But the fancy clothes for sale were out of the family's reach. "My mother was a seamstress and she made my clothes and took in sewing for other people to make a little revenue," she says. "Believe it or not, I made all my clothes too. I never bought a suit—a two-piece suit—in my life. I made all my children's clothes until they were old enough to get a job."

Little Larthy not only took to the kitchen but to her schooling as well. She excelled in her studies in the small blacks-only school she attended as a girl and the high school she graduated from in the mid-1950s. Her family had outlasted the Great Depression, and the economic surge during and after World War II provided the family enough uplift and money for Larthy to go off to college at Mississippi Industrial College in Holly Springs, located across the street from the well-known historically black college, Rust. For a farm girl from the hill country of Mississippi to go to college put her in an elite class of blacks in her home state and this surely was a source of great pride and admiration to her family. She decided early on that she wanted to be a teacher and she majored in Elementary Education.

Larthy had always found peace and community in her church and has been a devoted parishioner ever since she was born. The Rogers often walked from their family farm to the nearby Missionary Baptist church. The church was her home away from home, the church members a part of a loving, extended family who during those troubled racial times looked out for one another. A smart-alecky friend of hers told her that her church ways would trail away once she was enrolled at college in Holly Springs sixty miles to the north. Today she is very proud of the fact she never missed more than six Sundays of church during the entire time she attended Mississippi Industrial. Outwardly, Ms. Larthy does not come across as someone overly pious. But the fact that at 80 years old she still makes the drive from her Westwood subdivision in Memphis to Greater White Stone Church near downtown, a good 30 minutes away, once or twice every week even after she has retired as the church cook, says everything about what her church means to her.

courtesy Larthy Washington
Larthy Rogers at 23, fresh out of college and beginning her years as a grammar school teacher.

When Larthy Rogers graduated with her Elementary Education degree in 1959 she was quickly hired by a grammar school in Lambert, Mississippi to teach second grade. These were the days of segregation in Mississippi and this was an all-black school. Larthy lived in nearby Marks, Mississippi, home to some of the Delta's—and thus the world's—richest soil, making it ideal for large plantations of cotton. Larthy was in for a big culture shock moving from the hill country of Mississippi to the Delta.

"Quitman County, where I taught, was the poorest county in the entire nation," Ms. Larthy says today.

"The parents were unlearned. Some of the parents didn't even know their children's birthdays. 'Do you remember when Johnnie was born?' 'Well, let me see, I think that was the day it snowed…' Also they had what we called split sessions. Students would go to school for two months then be off for two months in the Fall to harvest on the farms. Then we would resume in late October." She taught there for six years.

One of the teachers in the high school building in the complex told Larthy that she had taught a young man that she thought she should meet. "That teacher just loved him from his head to his toes." "Well, where is he?" Larthy asked. "He's up in Memphis and I'm going to take you up there one day and we'll find him so you can meet him." And so she did. Cupid drew back his bow and let his arrow fly and before long Larthy was making frequent trips to Memphis and her new beau, Earl Washington, was making trips down to Marks, Mississippi.

Following a couple of years of courtship they married in 1961 and Larthy moved to Memphis to be with her husband. Earl worked for a paper company, a job that an uncle had helped him get. As Larthy tells it, "His uncle had migrated from the farm in Mississippi up north to Memphis to get off the farmland to get the better jobs. Many black people did this back then, and he got Earl a job in Memphis." Earl later worked for the Wonder Bread company making potato chips and eventually became a Building Engineer for Memphis City Schools, a secure job much valued in the Memphis black community. This was the job he would keep for the rest of his life.

Their first daughter, Kimberly Kay, who would be known by her middle name, was born in 1963. Larthy was a stay-at-home mom raising her one child and was contemplating working again once Kay was in school when the unexpected happened. Her name was Jennifer, born in 1970. "We would tell our baby child 'We didn't send for you,'" Ms. Larthy jokes today. "I didn't think I'd be having any more children, but it just happened," she says. "But I'm very proud of her."

Larthy and Earl had gotten married back in 1961 on a weekend. The next weekend her best girlfriend got married in Memphis. The weekend after that Larthy and Earl joined Greater White Stone Missionary Baptist Church and she has been a member ever since. "My husband's aunt was a member here and she just kept introducing me to everyone, and I guess we got stuck here," she says with a twinkle in her eye.

When her girls were small the family moved to the nearly all-white Westwood community in Southwest Memphis. Their friends thought they would transfer their church membership to the popular Mt. Vernon Church near Westwood, but they stayed loyal to Greater White Stone Church and made the long trip. "We'd put more gas in the car and come on over to Greater White Stone," she says.

Moving to the virtually all-white community of Westwood was bold risk-taking for the Washington family at the time. Unsavory real estate companies were "blockbusting," creating fear in white communities that ghetto blacks were moving into their communities bringing in crime and lowering property values. The hope was to get whites to sell cheaply and create a lot of sales and turnover in housing, increasing profits. And to an extent it worked. Lots of whites fled to lily-white suburbs.

Did the Washington family experience any prejudice or racial tensions after their move? "No, not really," Ms. Larthy answers thoughtfully. "You know, they were nice neighbors. My Kay's name is actually Kimberly. Do you know there were two other Kimberlys on our street? A big Kim, a little Kim, and a middle Kim.

They played together and just had all kinds of fun. They'd go back and forth to each other's house. In no time at all, once we moved there, everybody was normal."

By the time their oldest child, Kay, was in school, members of Greater White Stone Church all knew from pot luck dinners and visitations at her home that Ms. Larthy was a superb cook. As the church grew, naturally there were more members who died and the prominence of the church in the community meant there were a lot of funerals held there. For a long time church members were encouraged to bring pot luck dishes to provide food for the families in mourning. Often this did not suffice and the small dishes were quickly emptied during large funerals. The pastor at the time, Reverend Joseph McGhee, said "We need someone to do food preparation for these funerals." All eyes must have shifted straight to Larthy Washington. She told them that if the church were to appropriate the money for the food and pay her a reasonable fee for her time and trouble she would do it. It was a task she performed for the church for the next 40 years.

When her youngest daughter, Jennifer, went off to kindergarten, Larthy put on her apron and began cooking in earnest for the church. Funerals kept her busy at least three or four times per month cooking often for very large groups. "Black folks like to have their annual days, you know," Ms. Larthy says. "There was Ushers' Day, Grandmamas' Day, Grandfathers' Day, something like that all the time. Sometimes we would have special fundraisers for the church and sell tickets for the meal. I would cook for those too. I want you to know I did *all* my own baking. I never bought a cake the whole time I cooked.

"People ask me even today, how did you do it? Cook for all those people? And I tell them I don't know, I just did it.

"Every year they had a Baptist International Tea at LeMoyne-Owen College. All the Missionary Baptist churches across the city would meet for a special fund-raiser for LeMoyne-Owen College. Each church sponsored a table and would have food catered for their special table. I would be responsible for all the food served at our table. So people everywhere got to know my cooking.

"Of course, I got paid. But I didn't do it for the money. It was the enjoyment I got out of it. Ain't nothing I love more than cooking and watching the people sit down and eat it."

MS. LARTHY'S COOKING TIPS

Do you have a particular philosophy when it comes to cooking?

Well, I would say preparation before your cooking time is a good philosophy, so you don't have to rush into it and be doing something you shouldn't be doing. Preparation can make a lot of difference.

In many cookbooks I use, the cooks or chefs sometimes call for up to a dozen ingredients in a recipe. You, on the other hand, keep your spices very simple. You have a favorite trio: salt, pepper, and in many cases granulated garlic, which by the way I'm seeing more and more chefs specify in their recipes. Why do you use only those three spices?

Ever since I've been using them they come out tasty. What's the old saying? If it ain't broke, don't fix it (laughs). Yes, those are my three main ingredients, especially when it comes to meats. You may notice that sometimes I also slice up some onion and put it in the bottom of the pot and then add my meat on top.

Why do you put the onion in the bottom of the pot or pan instead of doing like most cooks and put it on top of the meat?

The steam and the heat bring the flavor up through the meat and it winds up with a better flavor.

You are mostly a self-taught cook, but I know you've seen recipes in books and magazines where the cooks and chefs call for a long list of ingredients. What do you say to that?

I say "what they needing that for?" This ingredient is the same as that and that one's the same as this other one. To me some of them serve the same purpose.

Do you think some people over-season food?

Yes, a lot of times. Sometimes when I go out to eat I get something and taste it and go "ooh, what is all this?" They got a lot of basil and this and that and it's to the point where you can see it all in the dish. It kind of turns me off.

Most cooks today seem to prefer butter over oleo margarine. You, however, call for a lot of margarine in your recipes. Why don't you use butter instead?

Hmm, I don't really know. I do use margarine in just about everything. The only thing I use butter for is when I do a pound cake. Even in my sweet potato pies I use margarine instead of butter, or if I cook candied yams. I've never been a butter cook too much even though growing up as I did out in the country we churned our own butter and it was there for every meal. My grandmother cooked so much rice when I was growing up and she put so much butter in it that sometimes the grains of rice would just be floating around in it in the plate, you know. And to this day I won't eat rice because of that. So I guess I just had my fill of butter.

As you know, one of my bad cooking habits is wanting to cook things too long, especially fried foods such as fried chicken and fried catfish. I use a laser thermometer to gauge my cooking oil, but you don't use anything—no thermometer of any kind. How do you know when the oil is the right temperature?

If you watch your oil after you put it in your skillet and turn on the heat it gets to a point where it appears that the oil is kind of dividing in a slow wave. It comes up in the middle of the skillet and kind of floats to the side. To me that's a good time to put in what you are frying.

How do you know when the meat, like chicken, is done and is at the proper brownness?

I guess it's your instinct that tells you. With fried chicken you need to turn it several times. When you turn it about that fourth time, it should be about ready.

A friend was telling me the other day that a lot of people make the mistake of getting a baking chicken instead of a frying chicken when they want to fry some chicken. That the baking chicken is plumper and doesn't fry as well.

That's right, a frying chicken is skinnier and more tender and fries up better. I believe that has something to do with the age of the chicken too. A baking chicken will be older than a frying chicken and a little tougher. The baking process softens it up.

A lot of people, including me, have spent some big money on cookware. What do you think about all those high-dollar name brands a lot of people use?

I just use an old country skillet. Not cast iron. I don't even know what it's made of. It's all right with me as long as it's big enough to hold what I'm cooking. I think these folks who spend all that money are a bit crazy (laughs).

So, it's not necessary to have expensive cookware to make good food?

I don't think so. I don't think it has nothing to do with the taste. If you look at the advertisements on TV it will make you think that, ooh-wee, if you put it in this pot here you just put it on the stove and put the stuff in and it's ready.

You chop your vegetables by hand. Have you ever seen the need for something like a food processor?

Yeah, I have one. But while I'm getting the processor out and washing it and setting it up I can have the vegetables already cut up. My children think I'm crazy. They say, "Mama, why you wasting all that time cutting up all that?" and I'll have it all cut up and in the pot and done and ready to eat while I'm setting up that food processor.

What about kitchen knives? That's something else people spend a lot of money on.

A friend of my daughter, her father made knives. One day he sent me three knives. Now that's been at least 15 years ago and two of them I've still got and use them all the time. One is a butcher knife and one is a paring knife. But they cut like a razor. Those are my two favorites.

What is something in your kitchen you just can't do without?

A mixer. For many years I used a basic mixer—I don't remember the brand—that cost only about forty dollars or so. My niece gave me one of those expensive Kitchen Aid mixers and that's what I've been using now for a long time. It's a real good one.

I'm sure most folks throw out their cooking oil after they've used it, but I notice you always save your cooking oil. I'm guessing you reuse it. How many times can you reuse oil?

I'm thinking you can use it about three times. Now if it's a long span of time between uses, you'll need to throw it out. But if you use it within about a month it will be good. You could go to the poorhouse if you bought it new every time you cook.

You've been cooking since you were just a girl. Can you think of what your most memorable meal would be?

That would be my Christmas dinner.

One special Christmas or all your Christmas dinners?

Every year, because I cook basically the same thing every Christmas. I cook a turkey and buy a ham. I cook greens, peas, potato salad, candied yams, plain cake, and sometimes I make homemade ice cream.

What dish are you most famous for? The one that people keep calling on you to make?

A lot of people love my coconut cake. And they love my potato salad too. I have people calling me asking "Can you make me some potato salad? Would you make me a coconut cake?"

Here in the church kitchen you cook on a gas stove. But at your home you cook on an electric stove. Do you have a preference for one over the other?

The only reason I would prefer electric over gas is because with an electric stove top you don't have to worry about all that food stuff falling down all over the burners where you have to clean it out and all. I don't find that one cooks any better than the other.

A lot of chefs and cooks are purists who believe in making everything from scratch. You, on the other hand, don't seem to have a problem using ready-made items from the grocery store in your recipes. For example, I'm thinking of how you use Pillsbury biscuit dough for your fried pies. Do you do this mostly for convenience?

I don't think it really tastes any different. It's handy. You just go and get a can of biscuits. Now that my hands are in such bad shape from arthritis I don't know if I could even make dough any more. I tell folks about the arthritis pains I get in these fingers that when they (the pains) come they bring the whole family.

How much experimentation do you do in the kitchen? You seem to come up with a lot of ideas that are strictly your own. For example you thought it up yourself to blend Mango Tang with instant tea to make your special tea and that is just a fantastic pairing of flavors.

Sometimes I just sit and think and put things together in my head, and then I'll try it. I program my mind before I even start something. Another idea came to me with my banana pudding. Now I've made banana pudding down through the years. But it would always be one or the other—it would be too soupy or too stiff. I couldn't really figure out what was going wrong. One day I went to get some bananas and I saw this banana pudding filling in a plastic tube (Concord Banana Creme Flavored Pudding & Pie Filling—*ed.*). I thought to myself if I mixed that with some Jell-O Instant Banana Pudding Mix I might get something that was really smooth with the texture just right and it ought to be really good. So I tried it, and everyone who I made that banana pudding for, before I'd get home the phone would be ringing with people asking "What did you put in that banana pudding?" They really loved it.

Are there any dishes you don't particularly like to make?

(Takes a moment to think) Well, sometimes when I make a cake and have to put the frosting on it I say to myself, "If I didn't have to put this frosting on here everything would be okay." Sometimes it's too soft or not soft enough and then you have to rassle with it. I always make my own frosting, you see. If it's too soft sometimes the cake might want to slide off.

What does the term "soul food" mean to you?

I think what it means is the type of food black people like to eat. That simple. And I don't like to fan my tongue so I don't put hot to it the way some folks do.

MAIN ATTRACTIONS (MEAT AND POULTRY)

SUNDAY DINNER FRIED CHICKEN

It is the best of dishes, it is the worst of dishes. Fried chicken when cooked with know-how and skill is one of the great wonders of the culinary kingdom. But when a beginner (I'm looking at my reflection here) with little skill or finesse gets hold of the world's most universal meat, watch out. Things can go wrong in a million ways. Let me count them.

Far too many cooks overcomplicate the basic recipe needed for outstanding fried chicken. Some people brine their chicken, some soak it overnight in buttermilk, some dip their chicken in an egg-and-milk bath before dredging in flour, some remove the skin before frying (there should be a cooking commandment against this horror), and some people double-dip into an egg-type wash. I have tasted some superb fried chicken all over the world that uses some of these techniques. If you have a family-tested recipe that you love and that has been passed down by your forebears, why change it?

But unless you've perfected the techniques above, you are likely to botch one of the great American dishes. I should know. I've tried almost all of those techniques and ruined countless batches of chicken. Brining and particularly dipping into a wash can make a tasty coating, it's true, but as Ms. Larthy explains it won't hold to the chicken. One bite and the coating and skin can scoot right off. "All that never did me no good with chicken," Ms. Larthy adds.

Ms. Larthy also doesn't believe in over-spicing. If Kentucky Fried Chicken is your go-to fried chicken and you have become accustomed to those 11 (count 'em) secret herbs and spices then your tastebuds have been hijacked.

Ms. Larthy seasons her chicken with salt, pepper, and her secret weapon, granulated garlic that is a coarser more meal-like version of garlic powder. That's it. Then she shakes her chicken pieces in flour. The flavors are wonderful but considerably more subtle than fast food fried chicken. This is Sunday dinner family-around-the-table fried chicken and should be enjoyed and respected as something home-cooked rather than store bought.

Post script: I have saved a recipe for fried chicken that appeared in a 1970s issue of *Esquire* magazine written by food writer Jim Villas. It's so old that it was photocopied on that awful greasy paper copying machines used to use. Now, Jim Villas knows his chicken and I'd accept an invitation to sit at his table any time. But his over-elaborate fried chicken recipe calls for a fresh-killed country-walked chicken (where you gonna get that in Manhattan?), a home fire extinguisher (I'm not kidding), milk to soak the chicken in overnight, and lemon (LEMON!) to add to the milk wash. He spends several paragraphs just telling you how to cut up a fresh-killed chicken. And several more pages telling you how to fry that chicken. I tried the recipe years ago. The chicken was a soggy, sodden mess and I didn't have a fire extinguisher, but needed one. I survived.

Let's let Ms. Larthy tell you how to do it right.

1 whole frying chicken cut into pieces
*Ms. Larthy prepared 3 chicken thighs and 7 breast strips for our cooking lesson

salt
pepper
granulated garlic
5 cups vegetable oil
4 cups all-purpose flour

Preparation:

Lay chicken pieces on a large square of aluminum foil, about 2' x 2' in size. Sprinkle well on both sides with salt, pepper, and granulated garlic. Put flour in two brown lunch bags (one inside the other for extra strength) and one-by-one put each chicken piece in bag to shake and thoroughly coat. (Note: I use a gallon size plastic Ziploc bag for this.) Heat oil in a large, heavy skillet. (Ms. Larthy uses an age-worn, heavily-encrusted skillet that looks as if it's seen 1,000 good meals). When temperature reaches about 375 degrees put in chicken pieces skin up. Turn pieces about every five minutes. Cook until a wonderful medium golden brown. Smaller pieces may be done in around 15 minutes; larger pieces such as thighs may be done in around 20 minutes. Drain well on paper towels before serving.

Cooking tip: As a student of cooking and certainly no master, I have a terrible tendency to overcook fried foods. Fried chicken, for example, is something I too often cook to a deep, dark brown instead of taking it off the fire when it reaches a sensible medium brown. Perhaps because many of us are used to that very deep brown of KFC chicken, which is not pan-fried but deep-fried and pressure-cooked, we think our home-cooked fried chicken should look the same as the Colonel's. Overcooking not only toughens the meat, it reduces the subtleties of seasoning and flavor. So rather than letting that chicken get a deep Florida tan, remove it when it gets a little Atlantic City browning.

BAKED CHICKEN

1 baking chicken
1 onion cut into slices
salt to taste
black pepper to taste
granulated garlic to taste

Preparation:

Wash chicken. Season well with salt, black pepper, and granulated garlic. Place onion slices in bottom of baking pan. Place chicken on top of onion slices. Bake uncovered for 2 hours at 350 degrees or until chicken is fully done. (Bigger chickens obviously will take longer.) Recipe works also for chicken pieces, which will take 1 ½ hours in oven.

FRIED PORK CHOPS

Susan Steffens

Note: Ms. Larthy reuses her cooking oil. For this pork chop recipe she used the leftover oil from cooking her fried chicken. Oil used to cook fish, you should be warned, cannot be reused because it imparts a foul, fishy taste to other foods.

8 pork chops about ½" thick
3 cups all-purpose flour
vegetable oil
salt
pepper
granulated garlic powder

Preparation:

Coat both sides of pork chops liberally with salt, pepper, and granulated garlic. Put flour in brown lunch sack or other suitable bag for shaking. Put chops one by one into sack, shake, and make sure chop is fully coated in flour. In a large, heavy skillet such as cast iron, heat about ½" of vegetable oil over medium flame until it reaches 350 degrees. Place about three or four chops in skillet (if skillet is large enough) making sure not to overcrowd the chops. There should be ample space between each chop. Do not turn over in skillet until the bottom of chop is well-browned. Cook in batches until all are cooked. Unlike chicken or fish, chops can be safely cooked to a deep brown color (in my many kitchen failures, I've found that it is best to remove chicken and fish when medium brown, not dark, golden brown) and not lose flavor. Drain well on paper towels or brown grocery bags.

SMOTHERED PORK CHOPS

If you want to take your fried pork chops a step further, "smothering" them with vegetables and allowing them to tenderize under a slow, low flame produces a wonderful mouth-watering variation. The vegetables, seasonings, and beef broth make a superb gravy that goes good with either cornbread or French bread. Or you can put the chops and gravy over rice. This recipe works well with round steak or flank steak too.

1 tsp. black pepper
½ tsp. white pepper
1 pinch red pepper
3 medium onions chopped
1 ½ bell peppers chopped
2 stalks of celery chopped
1 tsp. minced garlic
1 cup beef broth
1 tsp. of oil left over from frying the pork chops

Preparation:

Fry pork chops as described in previous recipe. Leave 1 tbl. of oil in skillet or dutch oven. Add half of all vegetables and seasonings and over low heat stir together and allow to cook for 10 minutes. Add the pork chops to the skillet or dutch oven and cover with the other half of ingredients. Cover and cook on low for about 1 ½ hours until chops are tender and ingredients make a gravy.

MS. LARTHY'S OVEN-BAKED PORK CHOPS

2 or 3 medium-sized pork chops
salt
pepper
granulated garlic
1 onion cut into slices

Preparation:

Wash chops and season as desired. Place onion slices in bottom of baking pan. In a skillet brown chops on both sides in a tablespoon or so of vegetable oil. Place browned chops in pan on top of sliced onion. Drizzle leftover oil and drippings over pork chops. Cover pan with foil and cook at 350 degrees for 2 ½ hours.

TURKEY NECKS
Recipe by Dana Merriweather

The lowly turkey neck, an outcast among meat parts, has nearly quadrupled in price in the past ten years in part because this dish that didn't get no respect all of a sudden has its place at the well-dressed soul food table. The reason should be obvious: when properly cooked, turkey necks are flat-out delicious. And if you know how to select them, they aren't scrawny little meat scraps either. Two turkey necks served along with a few good side items make a satisfying meal.

I was introduced to turkey necks by my former girlfriend, Dana Merriweather, who is quite a good soul food cook herself. As she tells it, she grew up literally poor and hungry in one of Memphis' toughest neighborhoods, and knew how to put together a tasty meal out of the least bit of groceries. I was initially hesitant to try turkey necks; after all they don't *sound* that appetizing do they? But once I smelled the wonderful vinegary aroma of those meaty necks simmering in a spicy bath on Dana's stove top, I had to give them a go and was very pleasantly surprised at how tender and delectable they were.

Dana tells me that it is imperative to get fresh turkey necks from the best grocer you can. She warns against getting frozen ones or the pre-cooked smoked ones. Pick the turkey necks with the most meat on them and make sure they have a vivid pink color, indicating freshness. Turkey is a rather bland meat that must be livened up with a lot of spices. This recipe, as you will see, calls for a good bit of spice plus the extra tang of apple cider vinegar. These flavors marry very well with the turkey meat.

1 cup chicken broth
2 cups water
½ cup apple cider vinegar
1 tsp. black pepper
½ tsp. seasoned salt
½ tsp. sea salt (or regular salt)
½ tsp. garlic salt
1 heaping tbl. garlic, chopped

Dana Merriweather when she isn't cooking.

Preparation:

Rinse turkey necks and remove as much as possible of any thin outer membrane you find covering the neck meat. Put all ingredients in either a Crock-Pot or sturdy 4 qt. or so pot. If in a Crock-Pot, cook on high for 4 hours. If in a regular pot, bring to a boil then slowly simmer for 2 hours.

Excellent served with cornbread and your favorite beans.

PORK NECKBONES

In case you are wondering, turkey neckbones and pork neckbones are two distinctly different dishes with entirely different flavors. Turkey neckbones require a great deal of seasoning and a vinegar broth to give them that punch of flavor that makes them delectable. Pork neckbones, like spare ribs, contain a small but very succulent amount of pork meat. You have to pick the meat off the bones (yes you can use your fingers) and it amounts to a sliver here and a sliver there. But good, very good.

Ms. Larthy told me, "I don't eat no necks. I don't eat no feet." And then she covers her mouth and laughs naughtily. "And I don't eat no tail." Her late husband liked neckbones, so she made them for him.

1-2 lbs. of pork neckbones
salt to taste
pepper to taste
granulated garlic to taste
1 onion, loosely chopped
1 cup water

Preparation:

Season meat with all spices. Place loosely chopped onion in bottom of a disposable aluminum pan large enough to accommodate the neckbones. Add 1 cup water over the neckbones. Cover pan with aluminum foil and seal well. Place in oven and cook at 350 degrees for 4 hours.

OXTAILS
Recipe by Eliza Jubert

Oxtails are no longer from oxen; they are from beef cattle, the meaty part of a cow's tail. When properly cooked they are delectable and are yet another throwaway part that has become a staple of the well-laden soul food table. This recipe was given to me by Ms. Peggy Brown, the loquacious proprietor of Peggy's Heavenly Home Cooking soul food restaurant. Ms. Peggy loves her food and loves talking about food. She wanted to make sure everyone knows this is her grandmother's recipe, at least 100 years old, that was passed down to her.

2 packages of oxtails (about 8 pieces)
salt

pepper
seasoned flour
1 heaping tbl. of Lawry's Seasoned Salt
olive oil
1 onion quartered
4 celery stalks cut into big sections
1 bell pepper cut into big sections
6 medium white potatoes cut into big sections
4 carrots cut into big sections

Preparation:

Wash meat well and season to taste with salt and pepper. Roll in seasoned flour. Heat an inch or so of olive oil in black skillet. Add oxtails and cook over medium flame until lightly browned. Add oxtails (but no leftover olive oil) to a dutch oven or suitable pot with lid. Add Lawry's Seasoned Salt, onion, celery, bell pepper, potatoes, and carrots. Add water to cover. Bake 1 ½ hours at 400 degrees. Check occasionally and add up to 2 cups more water if juices are getting low.

THE GAY HAWK RESAURANT'S PEPPERY HAM SHANKS
Recipe by Terica Bobo and Georgia Noel

Tom Graves

One of the oldest establishments in Memphis that is known for its soul food is the Gay Hawk Restaurant, built in the 1950s and bought by the Bobo family in the early 1960s. At various times it was known more as a bar and nightclub, but people still went there for the food. Terica Bobo, the daughter of the original owner, has made the Gay Hawk more a daytime restaurant destination these days and folks all over South Memphis come there to eat, especially on Wednesday afternoon when they offer a buffet and musical entertainment.

One particular dish at the Gay Hawk has been the talk of the town—their Peppery Ham Shanks. Many people, including a former food reporter for our local newspaper, *The Commercial Appeal*, confuse ham shanks with ham hocks, which is a totally different meat part. A ham hock is the bony, fatty portion of the hog just above the feet. Ham hocks are great for flavoring dishes, but are too bony to eat. The shank is the leaner, much meatier part between the hock and the shoulder and ham sections.

Ms. Bobo and her long-time legendary cook, Georgia Noel, who is now in her eighties, together devised this simple but delicious recipe. It is way off the traditional soul food roadmap and is included in this book because to my knowledge it is unique. No one else anywhere offers Peppery Ham Shanks.

Many hog parts that were a staple of African American cuisine for generations, in part because the cuts were very cheap, are today hard to find at meat markets. You will need to seek out a very knowledgeable butcher for fresh, not smoked, ham shanks and have the shanks sliced to a thickness of about ¾".

This recipe calls for a liberal sprinkling of crushed red pepper flakes over the meat. You may think this would make the dish blazing hot, but by some strange alchemy, when combined with the water and celery it works more as a flavoring component than a heat inducer. I was surprised that the recipe is so simple and doesn't call for salt, pepper, onion, or any of the usual seasoning suspects. Which is why this is cooking genius. Impress your friends and serve up this dish at your next soul food dinner.

2 lbs. of ham shanks custom sliced to around ¾" thickness
crushed red pepper flakes
4 stalks of celery
water to cover

Preparation:

In an appropriately thick baking pan or dish line bottom with ham shanks. Liberally sprinkle crushed red pepper flakes over all ham shanks. Place four stalks of celery across top of the seasoned ham shanks. Add water to cover meat.

Cover baking pan or dish with aluminum foil. Bake at 385 degrees for 3 ½ hours. Serve with cornbread.

BEER CAN CHICKEN

Note: Outdoor grilling is a culinary art unto itself, and Ms. Larthy's grilling and barbecuing methods are relatively standard offerings, thus we haven't included any of those basic recipes for this book. In Memphis pork shoulder sandwiches and pork spare ribs dominate. It is not that easy getting a good barbecued chicken in this town and that is the only barbecue my parents grilled when I was growing up. Over the decades I have perfected a recipe for barbecued chicken that I learned from some of the barbecue team experts who come to Memphis to compete in the annual Memphis In May World Championship Barbecue Cooking Contest. For this recipe a tall-boy can of beer is inserted into the chicken and it sits upright on the grill. I have had several friends tell me my bird is the tastiest chicken they have ever eaten. Try it and see if you agree. P.S. If you would like a recommendation for the single best book on barbecuing Memphis style, get *John Willingham's World Champion Bar-B-Q*. The late John Willingham was a barbecue genius; I can't describe him any other way.

1 tall-boy can of beer
2 tbl. poultry seasoning
2 tbl. garlic salt
2 pinches black pepper
1 whole chicken
virgin olive oil
barbecue sauce (your fave)

Preparation:

Empty beer into a large mixing bowl. Cut out the inside of the top of the beer can with metal snips or utility scissors. Mix poultry seasoning, garlic salt, and pepper in bowl of beer.

Heat your outdoor grill or smoker to 275 degrees. (Note: The grill or smoker needs to be covered to retain heat and smoke.) Massage entire chicken with olive oil.

Pour half the contents of the bowl back into the beer can. Then top off to 1 inch from the top with the barbecue sauce. Place beer can on a solid surface and cram the beer can into the bird's lower opening. Its butt in other words. Be sure the can is completely inside the chicken.

Coat outside of chicken with remaining beer/seasoning mixture. Set chicken and beer can on the grill in indirect heat. Adjust legs so chicken sits upright. It looks crazy as all get-out sitting upright like that on your grill, but trust me, it will cook deliciously. Cover grill and cook till bird is well-browned and done.

Barbecue teams that enter the Memphis in May Barbecue Contest often set up a whole row of Beer Can Chickens just to attract the attention of passers-by. And boy do they ever look funny sitting and looking at you like that.

MS. LARTHY'S OVEN BAR-B-Q CHICKEN

Memphis is the most bar-b-q crazed city in the world. If you don't believe me, just come for a visit. It is not uncommon to see hearty citizens manning a grill in the dead of winter, tongs and long forks at the ready. Not everyone can brave the cold winds and as a result another soul food variation became a comfort food staple: oven baked faux bar-b-q. No one wants to suggest it will ever take the place of smoked or grilled bar-b-q lovingly slow-cooked outdoors over hickory wood coals, but for a fast and relatively easy substitute it will deliciously get the job done.

1 3-pd. baking chicken
salt
pepper
granulated garlic
1 onion, sliced
sauce mixture: ½ bottle of hickory smoked bar-b-q sauce and ½ bottle of brown sugar bar-b-q sauce

Preparation:

Wash meat. Thoroughly coat chicken with spices. Place onion slices in bottom of roasting pan. Place chicken on top of sliced onions, cover roasting pan with aluminum foil and bake for 1 ½ hours at 350 degrees. Slather bar-b-q sauce mixture on chicken and bake for 10 more minutes. Allow to cool. Great with beans and slaw recipes in this book.

MS. LARTHY'S TWICE-BAKED MEATLOAF

Meatloaf:

2 ½ pds. ground beef
8 saltine crackers crumbled fine
1 tsp. salt
1 tsp. black pepper
1 tsp. Italian seasoning
1 tbl. sugar
½ cup chopped celery
½ cup chopped green pepper
½ cup chopped onion
1 8-oz. can tomato sauce

Meatloaf sauce:

1 8-oz. can tomato sauce
1 cup Worcestershire sauce
1 cup catsup
2 tbl. sugar
½ cup water

Preparation for Meatloaf:

In large mixing bowl, mix all ingredients together with ground beef. Mix well. Form into a loaf shape. Wrap tightly in aluminum foil and bake at 350 degrees for 2 ½ hours. Let cool, then refrigerate overnight. Remove from fridge and cut meatloaf into serving slices. Do not remove slices from loaf. Put loaf in aluminum baking pan of appropriate size. Ladle with a thick layer of sauce to fully cover meatloaf. Cover with a sheet of aluminum foil. Bake for 15 minutes at 350 degrees with foil on top. Take out of oven and remove aluminum foil from top. Bake another 15-20 minutes to fully heat and the sauce begins to crust slightly on top.

Preparation of sauce:

Mix all ingredients together well. No need to cook or heat.

LOVIN' IN THE OVEN BBQ PORK LOIN

1 pork loin, 3 to 5 pounds
salt
black pepper
granulated garlic
favorite barbecue sauce

Preparation:

Cover entire pork loin with generous sprinkling of salt, pepper, and granulated garlic. Rub into the meat well. Add a second layer of seasonings and do not rub this layer into meat. Refrigerate for an hour or so to let seasonings penetrate meat. Do not remove any fat from meat at this point; fat will help flavor meat as it cooks. Bake in a covered pan for 3 ½ hours at 350 degrees. Check to make sure loin is thoroughly cooked. Refrigerate at least four hours. Slice. Ladle your favorite barbecue sauce over loin. Wrap in aluminum foil and warm for 30 minutes in 350 degree oven. Serve while hot.

THE GREAT AMERICAN HAMBURGER

I'm with Anthony Bourdain all the way on this one: I can't stand gourmet hamburgers either. Or those things as thick as a hockey puck. If I walk into a fern bar and am offered a menu featuring a Kobe beef hamburger for twenty or thirty bucks I'm out of there like a shot. There are few food items in life as delectable to me as fresh ground beef slapped onto a sizzling hot grill that contains the grease of the ages soaked deep into the metal to give it an anointing of burger essence. The meat should get no more than a baby powdering of salt and pepper and that's it. If the griddle is appropriately hot, the outer layer of burger should wind-up crusted and seared, just enough to give the end result a bit of crunch and snap.

Remember in the old *Popeye* black and white cartoons (the best by far) made by the Fleischer Studios when Wimpy would order a burger and Bluto would slap a blob of burger meat on the grill and swat it down until it was a thin, burbling patty? When it was done he would flip it onto the buns, brush it all with a coating of mustard and Wimpy would wolf it down? That, dear reader, is how a burger should be grilled and eaten. Fancy is not a word that should ever be used in collaboration with the American hamburger.

A patty should be thin, certainly no more than ½" in thickness, and just big enough in diameter to slouch just beyond the edge of the bun. Bourdain likes catsup on his burgers. Nobody's perfect. A good, plain mustard like Gulden's is best. French's mustard, in my opinion, would be your worst choice unless again you decide to get fancy with a Dijon mustard, which is great on sliced roast beef but will murder a good hamburger.

Sure, once in awhile we all like a fully-dressed burger: with a slice of homegrown tomato, a leaf of good lettuce, a slice of Vidalia onion, pickles, and condiments. But a plain skillet-fried hamburger with a zingy mustard is just unbeatable. It is what 20th Century America thrived on.

Hamburgers grilled outdoors can be fabulous if they get a nice charry, smoky flavor. But nothing beats a burger cooked in an old, well-tested, well-seasoned cast iron skillet. Although I cast aspersions on highbrow hamburger buns, I want to caution you against buying the cheapest in the supermarket. Like buying a good locally-brewed beer, find a local bakery known for the best local sandwich bread. Their burger buns may cost you a little more than el cheapo brands, but will complete the holy burger trinity: burger, bun, mustard. Try it our way and see if it doesn't satisfy those cravings, save you money, and keep you away from those frozen patties soaked in ammonia that so many fast food chains use (don't even think I'm joking). Last, ground chuck (which is what you should get—you need fat to flavor the burger) cooked rare is not safe to eat. A burger should be cooked well-done to be sure any bacteria is thoroughly smitten, and I also don't think leaving it pink adds one bit of extra flavor. I know some would debate this, and that is their prerogative. I also advise leaving the burger to rest for at least a few minutes before serving to allow the juice inside to coagulate a bit and not run everywhere on first bite.

1 pd. of quality ground chuck to make 3-4 burgers
good hamburger buns (but not ridiculously fancy)
salt and pepper to taste
good, plain mustard

Preparation:

Preferably using a well-seasoned cast iron skillet, heat over medium flame. Form balls of ground chuck that are bigger than a golf ball, but smaller than a tennis ball. Put in heated skillet and using a spatula mash down until between ¼" and ½" thick. Add salt and pepper. Cook on bottom side of patty until you are certain a crust has formed and then when appropriate flip burger and cook thoroughly after again adding salt and pepper. Allow to rest a few minutes on paper towels. Put on buns, add mustard, and serve. By all means if you want catsup, mayo, or whatever suits your fancy, don't let me stop you.

DANA'S CHEDDAR WINGS
Recipe by Dana Merriweather

I have personally witnessed what happens when my former girlfriend Dana Merriweather sets out a plate of her Cheddar Wings. They disappear faster than you can say "Yo quiero Taco Bell." She takes a commonplace dish, hot wings, and by adding one little ingredient turns the recipe upside down and frowns right-side up.

Whole chicken wings (drummies work just as well)
Your favorite brand of hot sauce (not hot wing sauce)
A can of cheddar spray cheese

Preparation:

Fry your chicken wings using the recipe in this book. In a suitably sized Tupperware-type bowl with a lid, add about ¼ cup of hot sauce. Add about ¼ cup of the cheddar spray cheese and stir together well. Add one wing, seal lid on plastic bowl and shake vigorously to fully coat the wing. Remove wing, arrange on platter, and repeat with other wings. When the hot sauce/cheddar wing mixture is used up, simply add more. If you are doing many wings remember to have more than one can of cheddar cheese on hand because it goes quick. You will be amazed at how delicious Dana's Cheddar Wings are and yes, they are hot.

LET'S CHEAT A BIT CHICKEN AND DUMPLINGS

1 1.5-pd. package of ready-made dumplings (Mary B's brand was used for our recipe)
1 whole boiling chicken
5 quarts water
salt to taste
pepper to taste
granulated garlic to taste
1 can cream of chicken soup (optional)

Preparation:

Season chicken well. Boil chicken in large pot of water (5 quarts) for 40 minutes. Remove chicken from pot and allow to drain and cool. Remove skin then remove meat from bones and cut or chop into small bite-size pieces. Bring the leftover broth to a boil. Add the frozen dumplings broken to appropriate size if need be according to your desire. Drop dumplings in one at a time and stir, allowing each one to soften and absorb the liquid before adding another. If you have a preference for a thicker broth with your chicken and dumplings, add the can of cream of chicken soup. When all dumplings have been added and are properly soaked, cover the pot and reduce heat. Allow to simmer for 45 minutes, making sure to stir occasionally to unstick any dumplings. Add the chicken pieces and stir in well. Simmer for 10 minutes. Remove pot from heat and allow to stand for 10 minutes. Serve. You may want to grind some fresh pepper on top.

MS. LARTHY'S CHICKEN SALAD

3 pds. of chicken breasts
salt to taste
pepper to taste
granulated garlic to taste
1 cup chopped bell pepper
1 cup chopped celery
½ cup chopped onion
1 tsp. minced garlic
2 tbl. sugar (note: this may be reduced by half if less sweet is your preference)
6 boiled eggs grated
2 cups your favorite brand mayonnaise
2 cups sweet relish (note: I prefer dill relish—Tom Graves)
splash of hot sauce (optional)
splash of Worcestershire sauce (optional)
¼ - ½ tsp. celery salt (optional)

Preparation:

Season chicken breasts with salt, pepper, and granulated garlic. Boil chicken breasts in plenty of water for roughly one hour until chicken is well done and tender. Drain and allow to cool. Remove skin, then remove meat from bone and chop into very small pieces. In large mixing bowl, add all remaining ingredients. Stir and mix well. Refrigerate. When cold, it is ready to serve.

FRIED STEAK AND GRAVY

1 cheaper cut of steak such as flank steak or skirt steak (pork steak works well with this recipe also)
black pepper to taste
salt to taste
granulated garlic to taste
1 cup water

Preparation:

Wash meat. Season with salt, pepper, and granulated garlic to taste. Heat skillet. Brown meat on both sides. When browned, add water and cook on low flame for 30 minutes.

GRAVY

1 14.5-oz. can chicken broth
1 3-oz. package of brown gravy mix
1 ½ cups of flour
1 tbl. finely chopped onion
1 ½ cups water (if you have enough drippings left over from cooking steak add this with water to total 1 ½ cups of liquid)

Preparation:

Pour chicken broth into appropriate-sized skillet while skillet is cold. Mix flour and gravy mix separately with water and drippings and stir together well. Under medium flame allow chicken broth to heat up. Add onion to the broth and allow to cook and soften for 10 minutes. Using a wire whisk add the flour/gravy mix/water plus drippings to the skillet and stir well. Cook about ten minutes until thick while stirring frequently. Pour over steak and serve.

DOES IT SWIM?
(FISH AND SEAFOOD)

PAN-FRIED CATFISH FILLETS

Getting fried catfish to come out picture perfect is a skill that can take years to master. I should know. Only by working with Ms. Larthy have I finally been able to cook catfish to my satisfaction. Catfish, for decades, was considered a Southern delicacy best avoided by those who felt eating a bottom-feeding trash fish was unpalatable and déclassé. But when big agri-business stepped in and started farming catfish and feeding them with grain pellets, more and more people began to savor the mild and nutty flavor of cornmeal-breaded catfish fried in peanut oil. Very few people reported a fishy, muddy taste from farm-raised catfish. Catfish caught in the wild—well, that was another story.

There are outstanding catfish restaurants throughout the South today. My favorite way to eat catfish is whole, not filleted. If you have the right technique you can remove the meat from a side of the whole catfish in one fell stroke, and the meat will contain no bones. Delicious. However, getting a whole catfish pan-fried to perfection is much more difficult than cooking fillets. So, for me, I only cook fillets at home. I never eat catfish steaks. The reason is that in my opinion smaller catfish taste better than bigger catfish, which tend to be fattier, greasier, and retain more of that fishy taste none of us like. Whole catfish are smaller than the fish used for fillets (or steaks), so that's another reason I prefer the whole cat when I go to a catfish restaurant.

I have learned a few other tips about catfish I would like to pass along. I have been told that when you look at a catfish fillet, you will notice a brownish strip that runs right down the middle of the fish horizontally. That seems to be a hiding place for the fishy taste some folks report. So, using a fillet knife with a thin, sharp blade, remove that brown strip of meat. It's okay if in doing so your fillet becomes two fillets. Wash the fillets well to get any blood out of the meat. Then soak the fillets in salted water with the juice from a couple of lemons added for a few hours. This will get rid of any remaining blood and give you the best-tasting fillets.

I have read recipes that call for cooking at 375 degrees and Taylor Grocery outside Oxford, Mississippi claims to cook their bliss-inducing catfish at 325 degrees ("we cook it lower and slower"). I, and Ms. Larthy, cook ours at the traditional 350 degrees. Do not let the fillets overcook. Remove them when medium—not dark—brown.

4 catfish fillets, medium thickness, about 6" to 8" in length, preferably fresh, not frozen
salt
pepper
3 ½ cups peanut oil
3 cups yellow self-rising cornmeal

Preparation:

Lay fillets on a large square of aluminum foil, about 2' x 2' in size. Sprinkle well on both sides with salt and pepper. Put cornmeal in two brown lunch bags (one inside the other for extra strength so bag(s) will not break) and one-by-one put each fillet in bag to shake and thoroughly coat. Heat oil in a large, heavy skillet such as cast iron. When temperature reaches about 350 degrees put in fillets. Oil should almost cover the fillets but not quite completely. Turn only occasionally. Do not use fork to turn fish. Use a spatula or tongs instead. When a medium, golden brown take up and drain on paper towels. Should take 20-25 minutes to reach the desired golden hue. Do not let fillets get too dark in color as this will take away from flavor.

BBQ SHRIMP

BBQ Shrimp is really a misnomer. The shrimp gets nowhere near a grill or bed of coals. Instead, it is oven-baked in a bath of butter and savory spices. The dish gained popularity about three decades back when Paul Prudhomme's *Lousiana Kitchen* cookbook hit the best-seller lists and his version of BBQ Shrimp made it onto the menus of half of America's restaurants. His recipe is a good one; I've prepared it many times myself. It has become a staple of the well-prepared soul food kitchen.

At a dinner party several years back, I saw a heaping plate of BBQ Shrimp and added a few to my plate. When I tried them all kinds of bells and whistles went off. This BBQ Shrimp was even tastier than Prudhomme's version. So I asked for the recipe from my hosts and was told that the spice was made by the River Road company and available on-line through fiestaspices.com, which carries an assortment of top-line spice blends. As we've done elsewhere in this cookbook, we name the brand when that is what is used in a recipe's preparation.

My son-in-law, Jordan Buchanan, is a chef and was a chef/teacher at L'ecole Culinaire. I gave him a bottle of the River Road Barbequed Shrimp Seasoning and he loves the spice blend so much that he uses it in all kinds of dishes.

2 sticks butter
3 tbl. Worcestershire sauce
8 tbl. River Road Barbequed Shrimp Seasoning
2 to 3 pds. of de-headed, unpeeled medium to large shrimp

Preparation:

Melt butter and add Worcestershire sauce in shallow baking dish. Add shrimp seasoning and mix well. Add shrimp and mix well, making sure shrimp are fully coated. Bake at 350 degrees for 20 minutes. Shrimp should be pink around edges and well-coated with sauce. Serve with rice and lots of French bread to sop up the sauce.

SOUPS, STEWS, GUMBOS, ETC.

HOW TO MAKE AN AUTHENTIC CAJUN ROUX FOR THE UNINITIATED

Heavy 3 or 4 quart pot
1/3 cup of bacon grease (if you don't have any health issues)
1/3 cup of virgin olive oil (if you do)
1/3 cup of all-purpose flour

The key to almost every major Cajun dish is the proper preparation of a roux. A roux is basically a gravy base for whatever the meat or seafood happens to be, whether in a gumbo, a creole sauce, or an étouffée. This roux is specifically for a seafood-based roux. I always used bacon grease to prepare my rouxs until the day my cardiologist put me on a restricted diet and then I started to use the much healthier olive oil. Although there is a difference when using olive oil, I found it is very easy to season a gumbo to taste pretty much just like I want it. So, take your pick, bacon grease or olive oil. I don't recommend vegetable or canola oil. I just don't think they add flavor to the final product.

Keep this in mind when making a roux: it is a slow, tedious process. You cannot go off and leave it for even a minute. A roux that burns even a little bit must be thrown out. So it is best to go slow and do it right the first time. Also, it is wise to use a long-handled whisk or wooden spoon to stir (which you will do almost constantly) the roux while you are making it. Long handles keep your hands farther away from the hot grease, which when combined with the flour will stick to your skin and burn like napalm.

Make sure to start with a heavy pot. A thin pot won't do. You can prepare the roux in a thick sauce pan or cast iron skillet with the idea of pouring it into a bigger pot when finished. Over medium flame, heat your grease and do not let it get too hot. It does not need to be smoking or boiling. When it starts getting hot, but is not yet at the smoking stage, put in about a tablespoon of the flour and whisk vigorously until it is totally dissolved. When that is dissolved, add another tablespoon and repeat. Again, make sure you are stirring constantly. Repeat until all the flour is dissolved and make sure the roux is not browning too fast. If the roux is burned, dark speckles come into it. If that happens, sorry podna but you gotta throw that batch out and start over. Ayyyy-eeeee!!!

Okay, you've got the flour dissolved and you are stirring steadily but not crazily, just steady, lazy, daydreaming stirring. You will notice the roux slowly getting browner and browner. Keep stirring for what seems forever until the color is about as brown as brown (not tan) shoes. When it is a deep, nice, reddish brown take it off the fire and put in all your chopped vegetables as your recipe describes. Yes, when you dump it all in it will make an impressive "sssssss" noise and you will need to stir over flame all over again. Keep in mind that until you put those veggies in, the roux keeps cooking *off* the fire. So have those veggies ready to go in when the time is right.

Seasoned pros can heat up grease and throw in the flour without even looking, stir it up, and within a few minutes come out with a picture perfect roux. You can't. This takes years and I do mean years of practice in a hot kitchen. What *you* need to do is put on some comfortable shoes (don't do like me and cook without shoes on—Cajun napalm really scalds those little piggies and I have dropped a knife a time or two and hopped around bleeding all over the floor.) get a favorite beverage and stir, baby, stir. Put on a little zydeco or Steve Riley and the Mamou Playboys and learn the Cajun two-step while you are stirring. And, as always folks, *laissez les bon temps roulette!!!!!!*

ROUX MICROWAVE SHORT CUT

4 cup size Pyrex measuring cup
1/2 cup of bacon grease or other oil (vegetable, olive)
1/2 cup of all-purpose flour

Lou Ella Menard, the wife of Cajun musician D.L. Menard, who I talk about elsewhere in this cookbook, told me a long time ago that her preferred method of cooking a roux was in the microwave. I had heard it was kind of dangerous to use this method and that because the oil got so boiling hot you had to wear protective mitts to handle it.

I learned otherwise. You need a large 4 cup size Pyrex measuring cup and it is smart to use a good oven mitt or thick potholder to hold the handle of the measuring cup, but otherwise if you are careful you will do fine.

Make sure your bacon grease is good and melted down then add the flour and stir well. Put it in the microwave for five minutes, remove, and stir well, using a long handled spoon and being careful not to splash the very hot roux. Microwave for two more minutes, remove, and stir. By this time the roux is browning fast. I usually put it in for one more minute, remove, stir it very well and then slowly and with care pour the roux into a large pot. This roux should be a very dark brown. Have your vegetables ready and chopped and put them into roux. Stir the mixture all together well and proceed on with the rest of your recipe.

Mrs. Menard swore by this method and claimed, perhaps correctly, that the taste of the roux was better and lighter. I will say this—the microwave method is fast, easy, and saves a whole lot of time in the kitchen. It is now my go-to method. Try it.

TOM'S REAL KITCHEN SHRIMP AND SAUSAGE GUMBO

1 to 1 ½ pounds of jumbo shrimp (fresh is best, frozen will do)
2 hot dog-sized links of andouille or other good sausage, 12 inches if not in link form, cut into half-inch bite sizes
1 ½ yellow onions, chopped
1 bell pepper, chopped
2 big stalks of celery, chopped
1 or 2 finely chopped cloves of garlic (fresh if you are a stickler like Anthony Bourdain who abhors the minced garlic-in-a-jar, but if you're lazy like me, go for the jar stuff)
1 3-oz. package of dried shrimp, available from Asian grocery stores
1 tbl. Tony Chachere's Creole seasoning
1 tsp. black pepper
¼ tsp. white pepper
pinch of red pepper
½ Jumbo cube found in Mediterranean markets (Note: Jumbo is not merely a description, it is a brand name. Jumbo cubes actually are a bouillon cube, but they are ubiquitous in West Africa as a seasoning.)
4 cups seafood broth made using two Knorr Caldo de Cameron (Shrimp) Bouillon Cubes
7 or 8 shots of Worcestershire sauce
4 or 5 shots of your favorite hot sauce (optional)
2 shots of Liquid Smoke

Utensils needed:
A good heavy four-quart or so pot, not cast iron.

Preparation:

For me, few dishes stand so starkly chef-concocted as gumbo recipes. Restaurants all over America serve gumbo and they taste as if they all came out of the same pot. That's because they use the same industrial recipes and the same industrial ingredients for the flavor bases. Many of them also employ the use of fake crab meat, the Naugahyde of the culinary world. Really good gumbo is hard to find in Memphis. A five-hour drive down Highway 61 into New Orleans and you discover gumbo paradise. But absolute heaven is found in the small Cajun towns that expand out from the city of Lafayette. No two gumbos are the same down there, and they are all exquisite.

I have spent a good deal of time in the backwater towns of Acadiana. And every chance I get I talk to those people about their wonderful food. One of my most memorable trips was to meet the man they call the

Cajun Hank Williams, D.L. Menard. He wrote arguably the most famous Cajun-French song of all time, "The Back Door." Mr. Menard lived in a very humble country house with his wife, Lou Ella, in the little town of Erath. I was on assignment for the prestigious *Oxford American* magazine, and I was all set to interview Mr. Menard, my tape recorder and accoutrements at the ready. He and I sat and talked and talked and rocked back and forth in his hand-made rocking chairs and when I suggested we begin the interview, he waved his hand dismissively and said, "Oh Tom, we begin in a bit." I hadn't had lunch and was beginning to get uncomfortably hungry. Mrs. Menard excused herself and began preparing the family's evening meal. The aromas from that food were nearly wringing me inside-out. I thought to myself that I would surely faint from hunger if the interview didn't begin soon. Then it dawned on me. The Menards were preparing a table for me.

Mrs. Menard fried some red snapper, stirred-up a wonderful étouffée, and further prepared a salad, corn, and many other fixings. D.L. went into a back room and came out with a Crock-Pot filled with white rice. Exactly how they cooked rice in a Crock-Pot remains a mystery. This was most certainly one of the top ten meals of my life. Everything cooked right there in the kitchen, prepared by loving Cajun hands. Even the coffee, a chicory blend I'm sure, was some of the most slurpalicious of my life. Afterwards, I got a great interview with D.L.

Since gumbo *par excellence* is difficult to find in my hometown and very pricey when located, most of us Memphians over the years have turned to the late Chef Paul Prudhomme's classic *Louisiana Kitchen* cookbook; after all he was the king daddy of Cajun chefs. But you will be hard-pressed to find more complicated recipes anywhere outside Paris. It's not uncommon for his recipes to have 20-plus ingredients and require several days preparation ahead of time. For instance, Prudhomme goes to excessive lengths in the mere preparation of his seafood and other stocks. Because I am a faithful follower of recipes, I have collected crawfish heads after a crawfish boil and simmered them for hours, stinking up the house, just to have that perfect stock and get an imaginary pat on the head from the great Chef Prudhomme. Also, virtually every recipe in Prudhomme's book asks for palmfuls of black, white, and red pepper, a horse-choking combination of all three. Thus, to many sensitive palates, his recipes are inedible—flaming, burning, scorching, gimme-two-beers-quick hot, hot, HOT.

One day when I had a jones for a gumbo but was pressed for time I bought a box of Knorr's shrimp bouillon. I'll be damned if I could tell much of a difference between the bouillon and the Prudhomme seafood stock I had sweated over for an entire day.

Tom Graves

I discovered Jumbo cubes on a visit to Africa where they use this bouillon cube as a seasoning agent for meats. Jumbo cubes are available in many foreign markets in U.S. cities, especially African and Arab markets. This is one you might want to add to your arsenal of spices and seasonings.

I must give Chef Prudhomme one credit here, though. It was he who introduced me to dried shrimp, easily found at any good Asian market. These tiny little shrimp are used as a briny, robust flavoring and to add a bit of crunch to the gumbo. Preparation time for this gumbo—including making the roux—is one hour at the stove and another couple of hours of simmer time.

Making the dish

Prepare the roux as described elsewhere in this book. The gumbo must be prepared in a heavy pot, not cast iron. (Anthony Bourdain's rule of the pot needing to be heavy enough to kill someone if you conked them in the head with it seems about right to me.) Cast iron is great for nearly everything except soup-type dishes. Cast iron can impart a metallic taste to liquids that have simmered for long periods of time. My preferred pot for gumbo is a cast aluminum vintage Guardian Service pot with a glass lid. My first wife's mother, Lucille Maimone, used Guardian Service cookware exclusively and prepared fabulous meals with them.

When your roux is the proper dark brown color, immediately add all the chopped vegetables. Yes, it will make a wonderful "sssssssss" sound. Turn the flame to medium-low and let the veggies get acquainted, stirring frequently. After ten or fifteen minutes the veggies should be soft and form a mush-like texture. Cook a little longer if the vegetables aren't quite blended enough. Add the package of dried shrimp and stir into the vegetable mixture well. Add dry spices. Cook five to ten more minutes.

Slowly pour in the seafood broth you made a bit earlier (two boullion cubes dissolved in four cups of boiling water). Stir well. Add Worchestershire sauce, hot sauce (optional), and Liquid Smoke. Taste. If the gumbo is too salty at this point add two cups of water and extend cooking time. Add half the andouille sausage. (Note: The best Andouille sausage in the world is from Jacob's World Famous Andouille in LaPlace, Louisiana. My uncle lived in LaPlace and told me this. I thought he was exaggerating, bragging on his hometown favorites. But no, I finally stopped in there on a trip back from New Orleans and became an instant addict. This is the Beluga caviar of smoked sausages, believe me. They ship at reasonable cost, and I have ordered several boxes for Christmas presents. My relatives have loved me ever since. If you decide to order for Christmas, place your order before Thanksgiving. That's how popular they are.)

Bring to a boil and then allow to simmer covered on very low flame for two hours. Taste and adjust seasonings. You will notice that I do not call for salt in this recipe. The reason is because most of the other ingredients contain salt and the spice mixture called for should be sufficient in that regard. Again, if the gumbo is too salty, add two cups of water and let cook longer as described above. Add shrimp and remaining sausage. Cook for 15 minutes or until shrimp is just right. Serve with rice and crusty French bread or cornbread.

Makes about four hefty-sized bowls or eight smaller servings.

CHICKEN WING AND ANDOUILLE GUMBO

6 chicken wings
1 12" link of andouille sausage (polish sausage will substitute) cut into ¼" rounds
1 32-oz. carton of chicken stock
2 yellow onions, chopped fine
1 bell pepper, chopped fine
2 big stalks of celery, chopped fine
2 chopped cloves of garlic
1 ½ cups of chopped okra rounds
1 tbl. Tony Chachere's Creole seasoning
1 tsp. black pepper
¼ tsp. white pepper
pinch of red pepper
½ Jumbo cube found in Mediterranean markets (Note: Jumbo is not merely a description, it is a brand name. Jumbo cubes actually are a bouillon cube, but they are ubiquitous in West Africa as a seasoning.)
4 shots of Worcestershire sauce
4 shots of your favorite hot sauce (optional)
2 shots of Liquid Smoke

Utensils needed:
A good heavy two-quart or so pot, not cast iron.

Preparation:

Prepare and fry the six chicken wings as described in the fried chicken recipe in this book. When done, set chicken aside. Drain cooking oil from pot and reserve ½ cup and leave the pot scrapings in bottom of pot. Return the ½ cup of oil to pot and prepare a roux as described in this book using ½ cup of flour. The pan scrapings will add to the flavor of the gumbo. When roux is ready add all chopped vegetables except okra. Cook vegetables until soft, about 15 minutes. Slowly add chicken stock. Stir together well. Add ½ cup of the okra rounds. Using a food processor, grind the other cup of okra into a coarse but not too fine consistency and add to gumbo. (Note: This is a trick I learned from my Senegalese ex-wife, Bintou Ndiaye. Grinding the okra opens its flavor and thickens the gumbo.) Add seasonings, chicken, and sausage. Bring to a rapid boil, then reduce heat to slow simmer. This recipe does not call for any salt due to the saltiness of the ingredients. Add salt only after tasting if you feel the dish requires some. But be careful with it. Simmer for two hours and ladle over your favorite rice. Six servings.

BINTOU'S AFRICAN CHICKEN STEW
Recipe by Bintou Ndiaye

Tom Graves

My ex-wife Bintou Ndiaye was born in Sierra Leone, West Africa and fled to her father's home country, Senegal, in 1998 after her husband was killed by rebel forces who invaded their neighborhood in Freetown. We married in 2004 and I discovered what a wonderful, but reluctant, cook Bintou was. Living in the U.S. she would naturally get homesick for her native cuisine and would masterfully prepare elaborate West African meals, which I relished. A favorite dish was her African Chicken Stew which was hearty, reasonably spicy, and a proper fireworks of flavors. At a college where I taught they had an International Day and wanted faculty and students to bring a pot luck of as many foreign foods as possible. I talked Bintou into making her African Chicken Stew and dropped it off in the rec room where the International Day was taking place. An hour later I went to check on it and the whole pot was gone! I received several requests for the recipe. Here it is for you.

2 lbs. boneless skinless chicken breasts
½ tsp. salt to begin
1 tsp. black pepper to begin
1 ½ tsp. granulated garlic to begin
¼ tsp. red pepper to begin
½ Jumbo cube to begin
1 ¾ cups vegetable or olive oil
1 large carrot finely chopped
1 bunch green onions finely chopped
2 medium onions finely chopped

2 fresh tomatoes coarsely chopped
1 red bell pepper coarsely chopped
1 6-oz. can tomato paste

Preparation:

1. Wash chicken well and cut into cubes about 1" square.
2. Season chicken with salt, black pepper, granulated garlic, red pepper, and Jumbo cube in measurements described at top of page.
3. Heat cooking pot on medium flame.
4. When pot is hot, add vegetable or olive oil and allow to heat until near smoking stage.
5. Add chicken to heated oil. Cook to brown the chicken for 30 minutes stirring occasionally.
6. Remove chicken from oil when browned after 30 minutes. Set aside. Keeping red bell pepper separate, add all other vegetables to heated oil.
7. At this time add more seasoning to pot: ½ tsp. red pepper, 1 tsp. black pepper, 1 tbl. minced garlic, 1 tsp. salt, 1 ½ Jumbo cubes. Cook for 10 minutes partially covering pot and lowering heat to medium-low.
8. Add red bell pepper and tomato paste. Stir well.
9. After cooking 15 minutes add 1 ½ cups of water.
10. Cook for 25 minutes.
11. Add chicken that you have reserved and cook 30 minutes on low with pot fully covered.

Makes four to six large servings. Excellent served over rice.

CHILI COOK-OFF

My colleague at LeMoyne-Owen College where I taught for 14 years, Lydia Lay, and I for several years had a friendly rivalry over who cooks the best chili. Her recipe is entirely of her own devising and is a big hit with both her extended family, who insist on it for get-togethers, and those of us in the Humanities Building at LeMoyne. Mrs. Lay often brings a pan-full of her chili to pot luck gatherings on campus and she seldom has enough left over to scrape together a last meal of it. My chili, on the other hand, is true to the spirit of authentic Texas chili. No beans. No add-ons. We have been threatening to have a chili contest for a long time.

Enter Ms. Larthy Washington. I knew she also had a long-time recipe for chili that a whole lot of folks liked. I thought, why not bring all these chili recipes together for this book and compare and contrast them? One thing is for sure: chili is about as individualistic as a dish gets. No two chilis are exactly alike. Mrs. Lay and Ms. Larthy are both African Americans and bring a soul food twist to what is, by heritage, a Tex-Mex concoction favored by cowboys on cattle drives. Some folks think chili is a Mexican dish, but it is as American as Ms.

Larthy's Apple Pie. Just like with barbecue, there are regional identities to chili. Texas "red" is going to be very different from chili made, say, in Maine or in Alaska. And my Texas-style chili is very different from the two Memphis-style recipes from Mrs. Lay and Ms. Larthy.

TOM'S TRUE BLUE TEXAS CHILI

Isn't it curious how funerals and food seem to go together? At funerals in the South people bring food, lots of it. I've seen tables near collapse from the burden of all that food and you will seldom find someone so uncouth as to bring a bucket of chicken from the Colonel. No, people bring their best dishes and one of the few things that can help ease the pain of the loss of a loved one is a funeral banquet, where your mind can find something to be happy about, even if it's for only a moment.

My brother and I had to attend the funeral in East Texas of a beloved aunt. The little town was Pittsburg, Texas and one of the only notable places to eat there was a joint that specialized in hot links and crackers. Well, that sounded good enough for my brother and me and we agreed to meet up for a good lunch before heading to the funeral. We both noticed as we ordered that they had some mighty fine-looking chili too. So we added that to our order. Not only were the hot links spectacular, but the chili was some of the best I'd eaten since visiting Frank X. Tolbert's chili parlor in Dallas years back.

Authentic Texas chili has the consistency of pudding. The beef swims in a chili gravy of sorts. The beef is definitely there, but it is well-blended into the gravy. Some chili purists insist on cutting up a beef roast into small pieces and wouldn't think of using ground beef. But that's not only expensive, it's a pain in the rear to prepare too. To me and a whole lot of Texans, ground chuck works just fine.

True Texas chili also doesn't have beans. Or any other add-ons. It's a simple, straightforward dish and when properly fixed tastes fabulous.

I also believe that the secret of truly outstanding chili is the chili powder you use. Years ago someone alerted me to Gebhardt Chili Powder and all it took was one pot to convince me that this stuff was worth its weight in a conquistador's gold. Gebhardt used to be available in just about every grocery store, then there was a period where you couldn't get it at all, now it's available via mail order. I advise you to stay away from the run-of-the-mill brands you can get anywhere. There's a big difference.

1 lb. coarse ground chuck
1 lb. hot pork sausage (I favor the Jimmy Dean brand)
3 tbl. good virgin olive oil
2 tbl. butter

1 large bell pepper, chopped
1 large yellow onion, chopped
5 heaping tbl. Gebhardt Chili Powder
1 tbl. of really good ground cumin
2 tbl. minced garlic
1 tbl. salt
1 tbl. black pepper
½ cup all-purpose flour
6 cups water
1 8-oz. can tomato sauce
a few squirts of Lea & Perrins Worcestershire Sauce (optional)
1 tsp. of Tony Chachere's Creole Seasoning (optional)

Preparation:

Melt butter in a large metal pot. When melted add the olive oil. Brown the meat over medium heat. When browned pour off almost all of the grease and add 2 tbl. of Gebhardt Chili Powder. Stir into the meat well and allow the chili powder to sear into the meat without letting the meat scorch or burn. This should take only a few minutes. Add onion and bell pepper and stir in well. Next add in remaining 3 tbl. of chili powder, cumin, salt, pepper, and garlic. Stir well. Add in the flour a tbl. at a time until it is all mixed in with the meat. This will need to be stirred in very well. Allow to cook on medium-low temperature for five minutes. The meat mixture will at this point begin to stick to the bottom of the pot. Simply scrape it as best you can and stir into the mix. This will add flavor. Slowly add the water. Stir well. Add the tomato sauce, and again stir well.

The chili at this point will look much too watery. If you taste it, you won't like it. This now needs to cook down with the pot uncovered for two hours until it becomes that pudding consistency that makes Texas chili what it is. Over two hours the water will mostly evaporate and that reduction is when the flavor starts zinging.

After two hours, take the chili off the stove, cover and let it "sleep" for a day in the refrigerator. The spices will get to know one another. More than likely the chili will coagulate when chilled overnight. What I do to add some moisture is pour about ¼ cup of Tabasco brand Bloody Mary Mix into the chili, stir it well, heat, and serve. This is when you might want to adjust seasonings too. I usually add some squirts of Lea & Perrins Worcestershire sauce and a teaspoon of Tony Chachere's Creole Seasoning.

Many people like their chili spicy hot. If I'm speaking to you then you may add jalapeno pods to the chili as it cooks. Or you can add your favorite hot sauce to your chili before you eat it.

DI'S KICKIN' CHILI
(Add a pepper!)

Recipe by Lydia Dianne Lay

2 tbl. olive oil
1 lb. ground beef
1 lb. Italian sausage (hot or mild)
1 small onion
1 small can tomato paste
3 cans Bush's chili beans
1 can Bush's kidney beans
1 can Rotel tomatoes (hot or mild)
3 tsp. cumin
2 tbl. chili powder
Red chili powder, xtra hot Laxmi Brand (optional)
salt, to taste
black pepper, to taste

Preparation:

Saute onion in olive oil. Add sausage and ground beef, seasoning meat to taste with salt, pepper, and chili powder. Brown thoroughly. Add tomato paste, stirring throughout and let it burn (slightly!). Add two cans of water until water bubbles, stirring constantly. Reduce heat and add chili beans, kidney beans, and Rotel tomatoes. Add cumin and the 2 tbl. of chili powder. For hotter chili add the Laxmi Brand chili powder to taste, but be careful with it. Let simmer for 30 minutes and serve.

MS. LARTHY'S SOUL CHILI

½ lb. ground beef
½ cup chopped onion
1 tsp. black pepper
2 ½ tsp. salt
1 can of your favorite chili with beans
1 pack of your favorite chili mix seasoning
½ tsp. sugar
½ tsp. granulated garlic
1 8-oz. can tomato sauce

Preparation:

Brown meat. Cook on low heat 15 minutes to tenderize meat. Add all ingredients. Cook one hour and serve.

The results of the chili cook-off

The three of us all brought our batches of chili to the Greater White Stone Church kitchen. We each prepared bowls of our chili for the others to taste—a total of 9 bowls of chili for our tasting. We all enjoyed the three chilis and all agreed that each one had its own characteristics and interesting flavors. The zingy taste and seasoning of my Texas-style chili went over very well and the fact my chili has no beans or extras didn't seem to bother anyone too much. Lydia Lay's recipe also had a nice spicy bite, and was meatier than my recipe. I liked her blend of beef with Italian sausage; in fact, I may try that with my recipe next time I make it. The addition of beans to this hearty version gave each bite a chewy heft perhaps missing from my more pudding-ish style. Ms. Larthy's recipe, like so many of the things she cooks, is both utterly simple to prepare yet delights the tastebuds with complex flavors. I watch her and still don't know how she does it. I find it very interesting that she uses a can of chili with beans as a recipe starter and builds from that. Even though she used only a half teaspoon of sugar in her chili, I could taste it. It is amazing how even a few pinches of sugar can do miraculous things to a dish. Ms. Larthy's chili is the one most distinctively different from what most of us think of as traditional chili. I would definitely say that hers is a Memphis soul food version of chili and 100 percent delicious.

PRESSURE COOKER SPLIT PEA SOUP

An indelible childhood memory is of my grandmother in her kitchen cooking with her pressure cooker, the regulator on top of the pot vibrating with a ticking hiss of steam, making a most wondrous sound that portended delicious offerings. Pressure cookers fell out of favor by the 1970s, done in by mostly old wives' tales of the pressure cookers blowing up and scalding the housewives using them. There is a whole new generation of pressure cookers available today that have built-in safety valves that prevent any such occurrence. Even though they are totally safe, they haven't been embraced as devotedly as some of us feel they should.

Pressure cookers to me are like a Crock-Pot on speed dial. Soups can be prepared in a half hour. Beef roast in one hour. They save time and they save on energy. I'm still a novice, but I've noticed that you need to season more with a pressure cooker. I love split pea soup, especially in the winter, and I had to experiment quite a bit until I was satisfied with this recipe, and at this point I am confident enough to share it with you.

There are ingenious and pricey new pressure cookers on the market that allow you to "set it and forget it" as Ron Popeil so memorably told us to do with his rotisserie. I picked up a stove top model for around $20 on Amazon.com that works just fine. And I just love the sound it makes. But when I ran across a new-in-the-box Instant Pot at the Goodwill store for $25, I bought one. Now it has become a permanent fixture on my kitchen counter.

8 cups chicken stock
1 pd. dried split peas
1 ham hock
1 onion, diced
2 stalks celery, diced
1 tomato, chopped
1 tsp. minced garlic
1 tsp. dried thyme
1 tbl. ground black pepper
1 tsp. salt
1 tsp. hot sauce
2 bay leaves
1 tbl. Worchestershire sauce
½ tsp. Liquid Smoke
1 tbl. butter

Preparation:

In a skillet or sauce pan saute onion, celery, and garlic in a tbl. or so of butter. Add chicken stock to pressure cooker. Add all ingredients, including sautéed ones, to pressure cooker and stir well. Close pressure cooker securely as directed in your pressure cooker instructions. Bring to high pressure and when regulator is gently rocking cook about 30 minutes. When done pour cold water over pressure cooker to release pressure according to manufacturer's instructions. Remove ham hock, strip off meat and add to soup. Stir well to distribute flavors. Serve.

HELPFUL HINT: If you want a really smooth soup put it in a blender and puree. It will look beautiful.

MS. LARTHY'S LEFTOVER BEEF ROAST STEW

This is a fantastic way to take advantage of leftovers from a beef roast.

Leftovers from a beef roast cut into small pieces (or beef stew meat)
black pepper to taste
salt to taste (note: add salt only on your final tasting while cooking and only if you need it)
1 tsp. Tony Chachere's Creole seasoning
4 or 5 shots of Worcestershire sauce
2 shots of Liquid Smoke
4 or 5 shots of your favorite hot sauce (optional)
beef broth according to taste
1 small can tomato paste
1 can mixed vegetables
1 can corn
½ package of beef stew seasoning

Preparation:

If using stew meat, wash meat and while adding small amounts of water, cook stew meat in appropriate-sized pan until tender. If using beef roast leftovers simply add to your cooking pot. Add all other ingredients plus an amount of beef broth that is right for your taste. Stir well to disperse tomato paste. Add more beef broth if you like a thinner stew, less if you like it thicker. Stir well. On low heat, cook for 30 minutes. Excellent with cornbread or Mom's rolls. Also good using a slow cooker such as a Crock-Pot on low setting for the day.

EAT YOUR VEGETABLES

TOM'S WHITE BEANS AND RICE

Many people know red beans and rice. But Cajun chef Alex Patout, who invented the deep-fried Cajun turkey, swears by white Northern beans. I think they are better too. Why? They seem to absorb the seasonings better than red beans. Many people use dried beans and soak them overnight, but I just don't have the patience for that and on too many occasions the dried beans, even after a night's soaking, just don't want to soften up and stubbornly take several hours longer to cook than they should. So, if fresh-from-the-garden Northern beans are available, they are great. But I see no problem with using normal-sized cans of beans where they are pre-softened for you. Since sodium is almost always added to canned beans, I do not use salt at all in this recipe. I advise withholding any salt unless you taste the beans at least an hour into cooking and think salt is needed. But be careful with it.

Tom Graves

2 15.5-oz. cans basic white Northern beans (fresh beans are better if you have them)
Andouille sausage (or Polish sausage if that's all that's available)
One ham hock
One yellow onion chopped
One bell pepper chopped
Two stalks of celery chopped

Two cloves minced garlic
1 tbl. black pepper
1 tsp. white pepper
1/4 tsp. red pepper
Two bay leaves
2 tbl. Tony Chachere seasoning
2 tbl. Lea & Perrin's Worchestershire Sauce
Several squirts of the Asian hot sauce with the rooster on it (or other hot sauce)
Any other seasonings you want
Don't add salt—you probably won't need it
Part of the sausage cut into about a handful of ¼" rounds
Split a length of sausage (about as long as a regular hot dog) in half

Preparation:

Chop up vegetables. Dump everything in a thick-bottomed pot. Add cold water to cover two inches above everything. Cook over medium flame for about two hours until most of the water is gone and it's now a muddy, mushy consistency. Stir frequently and don't let beans burn on bottom.

Cook your rice, whatever type you prefer. An hour and a half into the beans cooking, split your length of sausage in half length-wise. Fry it up in a cast iron skillet, starting from a cold pan. I fry mine until the sausage has a crispy exterior on the flat side.

Make a pile of rice on your plate. Smother with beans on top. Place a half of fried sausage on each side of your plate. French bread or garlic bread go well with this. Savor!

MS. LARTHY'S EXTRA TASTY GREEN BEANS

3 14.5-oz. cans of cut green beans. Fresh green beans, of course, are best
1 large cube of hog jowl cut into ¼" slices
¼ bell pepper cut into ½" thick rings
4 slices of onion cut ½" thick
1 tsp. sugar
salt to taste (optional)

Preparation:

Pour off half the water from each can of beans. Put all ingredients together in a suitable cooking pot and mix well. Bring to a boil, and then reduce heat and cook over a medium-low flame so that beans slowly boil. Leave pot uncovered for first 10 minutes, then cover for remaining 15 minutes of cooking time. Stir occasionally, allowing flavors to shake hands.

BLACK-EYED PEAS

8 oz. of garden fresh black-eyed peas (frozen will substitute)
water
one ham hock or hog jowl
¾ tbl. salt
½ tbl. pepper
1 tsp. sugar
1 chopped onion

Preparation:

Cook peas over medium-low heat in water to cover with all ingredients (except onion) until peas are tender, about an hour and 15 minutes. A thick and tasty liquor should form towards end of cooking time. Add chopped onion and cook ten minutes longer. Serve. Although we don't have a recipe for chow-chow in this book, it goes great with black-eyed peas.

SOUL-STYLE BOILED CABBAGE

1 cup of "boiling meat"—hog jowl cut into small pieces or short strips
1 bell pepper, chopped
2 ribs of celery, chopped
1 large cabbage cut and washed
2 cups water
1 tsp. sugar
salt to taste
pepper to taste
1 tbl. olive oil

Preparation:

Cook "boiling meat" in bottom of a good-sized, thick pot in 1 tbl. olive oil. Once cooked, add bell pepper and celery. Allow vegetables to soften for 10 minutes. Stir well. Add cabbage and 2 cups water. Add sugar and other spices. Bring to a boil and let boil for 30 minutes. Allow to cool somewhat before serving.

HOME FRIES

2 medium Russet potatoes sliced to desired thickness
5 cups vegetable oil
salt to taste

Preparation:

Heat oil in large, heavy skillet. When oil temperature reaches 350 degrees put potatoes in skillet. Cook until a light golden brown, not a dark golden brown. Fries should be done in 8-10 minutes. Remove from skillet and drain on paper towels. Salt to taste.

*Note: Home fries may not be as crispy as those we typically eat at fast food restaurants. However, the flavor of the potato should be much more robust. The first time I ate at the renowned Doe's Eats steak restaurant in Greenville, Mississippi, where presidents come to dine, I was dismayed when I picked up a french fry and it drooped, kind of like a male's flaccid…well, you get the idea. When I bit into one, however, I couldn't believe the rich, sweet flavor of the potato which blended perfectly with the charry taste of the browned exterior. It was a perfect marriage of flavor and texture. These home fries will give you a close taste.

WHITE POTATOES WITH CHEESE

4 medium Russet potatoes
1 onion cut into slices
1 tsp. salt
black pepper to taste
½ stick of margarine
1 cup grated cheddar cheese

Preparation:

Peel and wash potatoes. Cut each potato in half. Place onion slices in bottom of cooking pot. Add potatoes, water to cover, and salt. Cook on low boil for 45 minutes. Drain water. Add black pepper to taste, margarine, and grated cheese. Allow to melt, then stir ingredients to properly coat potatoes. Arrange on platter and serve.

EL PERFECTO BAKED POTATO

Here's something else that I've found easy to screw up. How many of us have tried different methods of baking a potato only to have the potato half done and still crunchy inside? I learned to leave off wrapping the potato in aluminum foil; just oil it, salt it, throw it in a well-heated oven and presto!, out comes a perfect baked potato.

salt
olive oil
1 Idaho potato

Preparation:

Pre-heat oven to 400 degrees. Scrub dirt and grit off potato. With a fork liberally punch holes over the entire potato. Rub with olive oil and add a heavy sprinkle of salt over potato. Place in oven and bake for 1 ½ hours. DO NOT WRAP IN FOIL. When done the outer skin of potato should be nice and crispy (and edible if you like) and the inside should be light and fluffy and melt in your mouth.

SKILLET-FRIED CORN

10 ears of fresh corn
1 stick butter
½ cup water
1 tsp. salt
1 tsp. black pepper

Preparation:

Shuck corn and remove all silk. Wash well. Using a knife (be careful here) cut all corn from the cob directly into a large, heavy skillet (cast iron works great with this recipe). Using the blunt side of the knife blade, scrape the cob again to get the "milk" from the cob and let drip into skillet with the corn. Melt butter in skillet with the corn and when melted immediately add water, salt, and pepper. Over very low flame cook for 45 minutes. The corn should thicken dramatically by end of cooking time and should not be browned or scorched. If so, the flame was too hot. Let cool slightly and serve.

MS. LARTHY'S FRIED CORN ON THE COB

4 ears of corn broken in half
salt to taste
pepper to taste
2 sticks of margarine or butter

Preparation:

In a deep skillet or dutch oven melt 2 sticks of margarine or butter. Season the corn, then place in skillet or dutch oven and cook for 20 minutes on low heat, turning corn frequently to make sure all the cob cooks equally and evenly. Brown scorch marks will normally be present and visible on the finished corn. When done, drain for a few minutes and serve while still nice and hot.

SMOTHERED BROCCOLI

1 large head of broccoli cut into appropriate pieces
1 tsp. salt
black pepper to taste
½ stick of margarine
grated cheese to taste (probably about ½ cup will do)

Preparation:

Wash and drain broccoli. Place in cooking pot. Cover with cold water and salt. Cook on low boil for 15 minutes. Drain water. Add black pepper, margarine, and grated cheese to taste. Serve immediately.

OOH BOY BROCCOLI SALAD

1 large head of broccoli cut into appropriate pieces
1 pound bacon cooked and cut or crumbled in small bite-sized squares
3 small 1.33-oz. boxes of raisins (or 1 cup chopped pecans)

Sauce for broccoli salad:

2 cups mayonnaise
1 ½ cups white vinegar
2 ½ tbl. sugar

Preparation:
Mix ingredients well in mixing bowl. Slowly drizzle sauce over the salad. Mix well. Serve.

NOT TOO SLIMY BOILED OKRA

1 pd. whole okra (fresh if possible)
1 tsp. salt
1 tsp. pepper
1 stick margarine

Preparation:

Place okra in a boiler and add water to cover. Add salt. Cook for 30 minutes over medium heat. Drain water. Add margarine and pepper and simmer on low for five minutes. Serve.

HOLLERIN' FOR THEM COLLARDS (COLLARD GREENS)

3 bunches of collard greens
1 ham hock or hog jowl
1 ½ tbl. sugar (reduce sugar to ½ tsp. if you don't like it as sweet)
1 tbl. salt
1 tsp. black pepper
¼ tsp. crushed red pepper flakes
1 tbl. greens seasoning
3 tbl. bacon drippings
pepper sauce (on your table to use if you want to "kick it up" a few notches)

Preparation:

Pick through greens and throw out any that are not good. Wash greens well. Put ham hock or hog jowl in pot and add water to cover. Boil over medium flame for one hour adding water if needed. While meat is still boiling add the collard greens, cover with water, and add all other ingredients. Cook for 1 ½ hours. Serve.

FRIED OKRA

1 6-oz. or 12-oz. package of sliced frozen okra (fresh okra is fine too, of course)
½ tsp. black pepper
½ tsp. salt
cornmeal
buttermilk
vegetable oil

Preparation:

Season okra with salt and pepper. Dip in buttermilk to coat and then dredge okra through cornmeal. Under a medium flame warm 1/2" or so of vegetable oil in a frying pan. When oil is warm but not yet hot add okra. Make sure there is enough oil to just cover okra. Add more oil if needed. As oil heats, the okra will brown. When thoroughly browned remove okra from frying pan and allow to slightly cool. Serve while warm.

FRIED GREEN TOMATOES

Tom Graves

Fried green tomatoes and fried okra.

3 green tomatoes
½ tsp. black pepper
½ tsp. salt
1 ½ cups of buttermilk
cornmeal
vegetable oil

Preparation:

Wash and slice the green tomatoes. Season with salt and pepper. Dip in buttermilk, dredge in cornmeal, and add one at a time to heated vegetable oil in a frying pan. Fry until tomatoes are golden brown color.

BREADS

CORNBREADS THREE

If there is any single dish that differentiates between soul food and country cooking, it is one of this country's oldest foods, the American farmer's good old cornbread, begat when the first New World settlers understood what maize was all about from Native Americans and realized all its fantastic cooking properties and potential. Cornmeal was a lot easier to come by in those treacherous and hard times than wheat flour, so not surprisingly corn was the staple of many types of bread, whether they were called Johnnycakes, hoecakes, corn pone, or hushpuppies. Country cornbread is typically thought of as slightly salty, perhaps from bacon drippings and pork cracklins often used in the batter, a touch buttery, and most definitely not sweet. Soul food cornbread comes down to this: Is it "Jiffy" Mix or not? Because "Jiffy" Mix is nearly ubiquitous—in Memphis certainly—as *the* soul food cornbread and is hugely sweet. For people like me raised on country cornbread, "Jiffy" Mix cornbread is an acquired taste and requires a blood sugar check if you dive into it.

"Jiffy" Mix has been on America's grocery shelves since 1930 and is manufactured, not in the South as you might think, but in Chelsea, Michigan, of all places. Unlike cornbread made from scratch, "Jiffy" Mix is almost impossible to foul up. Trust me.

Ms. Larthy and I decided to cook three different styles of cornbread and compare them in a taste test. My entry is one I discovered several years ago on an index card in my Mom's recipe box. I'm pretty sure my Mom did not create this recipe but got it from some now anonymous source that I cannot trace. After trying it, this recipe has become my go-to cornbread. For me it is nearly foolproof. This recipe is very buttery, savory, and has a delicacy to it that many other cornbreads do not.

Ms. Larthy's recipe is, as can be seen, made utterly from scratch. This is the recipe she has used her whole life.

MS. LARTHY'S GOOD & GRAINY CORNBREAD MUFFINS

Susan Steffens

(makes six muffins)
1 ½ level cups Aunt Jemima Self-Rising Cornmeal
1 large egg
½ cup whole milk
¼ cup water
vegetable oil

Preparation:

1. Preheat oven to 350° (Note: this is a lower temp than most cornbread recipes call for. You may want to experiment with the temp at 400°).
2. Mix all ingredients well in large mixing bowl.
3. Put ¼ tsp. vegetable oil in each muffin mold.
4. Pour batter into each muffin mold and bake for 30-35 minutes or until golden brown.

MOM'S INDEX CARD CORNBREAD

Susan Steffens

1 cup plain yellow cornmeal
1 cup all-purpose flour
1 tbl. baking powder
1 tsp. kosher salt
¼ tsp. baking soda
2 cups buttermilk
2 large eggs
½ cup butter

Preparation

1. Preheat oven to 425°. Whisk together first 5 ingredients in a large bowl. Whisk together buttermilk and eggs; stir into cornmeal mixture just until combined. Heat a 10-inch cast-iron skillet (or dutch oven) over medium-high heat until it just begins to smoke. Add butter, and stir until butter is melted. Stir melted butter into cornbread batter. Pour batter into hot skillet.

2. Bake at 425° for 25 to 30 minutes or until golden and cornbread pulls away from sides of skillet. Invert cornbread onto a wire rack; serve warm.

"JIFFY" CORNBREAD

Instructions as printed on "Jiffy" Mix 8.5-oz. package

1 8.5-oz. pkg. of "Jiffy" Corn Muffin Mix
1 egg
1/3 cup milk

Preparation

1. Preheat oven to 400°.

2. Grease muffin pan or use paper baking cups. (Note: You can also use a cast iron skillet or other type of baking pan that is suitable.)

3. Blend ingredients. Batter will be slightly lumpy. (For maximum crown on muffins let batter rest for 3 or 4 minutes, stir lightly before filling cups.)

4. Fill muffin cups 2/3 full.

5. Bake 15-20 minutes or until golden brown.

Our Taste Test Results

Since Ms. Larthy has been perfecting her recipe since she was old enough to milk a cow, naturally that is a taste she favors. I liked her cornbread muffins very much, even though I prefer wedges of cornbread sliced from a round loaf rather than muffins. I found her recipe pleasantly unsweet with a very, very slight saltiness. The benefit of her recipe is a distinctly nutty flavor where the cornmeal texture—its graininess—is very prominent. Those who like whole grains and enjoy the mouth feel of coarser meal will appreciate Ms. Larthy's version. Ms. Larthy was quite taken with my Mom's recipe, which I got off an index card in her recipe box, noting the smooth texture and buttery taste. Like me Ms. Larthy prefers a less sweet cornbread. Neither of us particularly likes "Jiffy" Mix. It, to both of us, more resembles cake than our ideal cornbread. But it has its plusses. It is easy and quick to bake and as stated is almost guaranteed to come out right. The sweeter taste can balance out other saltier foods, such as fried chicken and fried pork chops. "Jiffy" Mix also has a superbly fine mouth feel and an almost perfect level of chewiness.

MY BEST (SO FAR) BUTTERMILK BISCUITS

The most difficult dish in this book by far is for buttermilk biscuits. Ms. Larthy doesn't even bother with them and hasn't for years. "That's too much like work making biscuits," she told me early on. Indeed.

If the least thing is wrong in your preparation making biscuits, they won't turn out right. There's a nice lady on Youtube with a video of her making a batch of biscuits and she admits that it took her two years—TWO YEARS!—to perfect her recipe. I tried her recipe and for me it was a fail. There are people who insist on using frozen butter grated into the flour in their recipes. Some use lard. Most use Crisco shortening. Some folks use all-purpose flour and add Clabber Girl Baking Powder and others use self-rising flour. Most authoritative biscuit makers swear by White Lily brand flour and the fact it is a soft winter wheat. Some people use whole milk, most use buttermilk. A few connoisseurs claim aged buttermilk works best.

Almost all of these recipes, and I've tried many, turn out a biscuit that is doughy in the middle, too crusty on top and sides, and way too hard on the bottom. A good biscuit should be lightly browned on top and buttery, with a slight taste of salt in the mouth, which is perfectly offset by the sweetness of jams, jellies, syrup, and molasses. Not to mention how well it goes with gravy. Biscuits should be airy and fluffy in the middle with no sign of doughy-ness. The bottom should be well-browned with a thin and crispy crust.

My gold standard for biscuits is those made by my maternal grandmother. They met all the above criteria and then went the extra mile. The biscuit tops weren't just crusty; they were delicious brown caps that gave way to a chewy, fluffy heaven inside. These biscuits stuck to the ribs and were not as aerated and airy as many biscuits. The bottoms were perfectly crisp and crusted. My brother and I begged our Mom to learn Grandmama's recipe, but she wasn't the least bit interested. Too much like work I guess. When I was 14 years old and just beginning to reach the age when I could fully appreciate my Grandmother's talents in the kitchen she passed away. And she took her biscuit making with her.

A decade or so went by and I discovered a new bar-b-q joint around the corner from where I lived in Memphis. They advertised their "country breakfasts" and one morning I decided to give the breakfast a shot. To my amazement the biscuits were EXACTLY like my Grandmother's. Calling these biscuits comfort food doesn't begin to describe what they meant to me or how they helped me recapture a treasured taste from my past. The restaurant is Bryant's and they don't even serve bar-b-q anymore. But their breakfasts—and biscuits—are famed all over the South. Over the years I've become friends of the brother and sister who now own and run Bryant's, named after their father who founded the restaurant. They know I want their biscuit recipe. As I write this they still have my request under consideration. I can certainly understand why a restaurant would want to keep their prized recipes to themselves. We'll see how it plays out.

After a great deal of experimentation and a lot of inedible batches of biscuits, the one I provide here seems to be a failsafe recipe, at least for me. I must say this is by far the best biscuit recipe I've tried in my own kitchen. After my first batch I could not stop eating them. Delicious!

While these are *not* my Grandmother's biscuits, they are still excellent. Just for the record, the best biscuits I've ever eaten—better even than my Grandmother's—were at Earl's Hot Biscuits restaurant in West Memphis, Arkansas. I remember taking rock critic Dave Marsh there for breakfast when he was in town and how bowled over he was by the biscuits and his first go (as I remember it) at some authentic red-eye gravy. Earl's has been closed now at least a decade. I've been wheeling and dealing with some of the powers that be in West Memphis to track down that recipe. Again, we shall see.

Until I get Bryant's and Earl's biscuit recipes, give this one a try.

2 cups White Lily self-rising flour
Heaping ¼ cup of Crisco vegetable shortening
¾ cup full fat buttermilk and maybe up to ¼ cup more if needed

Preparation:

Preheat oven to 500 degrees. In a proper bowl mix the shortening into flour with fingers until dough is nice and crumbly. Pour in the ¾ cup of buttermilk and stir until dough forms into a rough ball. Pour in a little more buttermilk if a lot of flour is left in bottom of bowl. Dust countertop or chopping board with flour. Take ball of dough and press and pat dough until it is in a rectangular shape and about 1" thick. Do not knead dough and try your best to keep it at 1" thickness. Using a biscuit cutter cut out your biscuit rounds. Place biscuits into greased pan or cast iron skillet or baking tray with biscuits all touching. Pour 3 tbl. of melted butter onto biscuit tops. Bake for 15 minutes until tops are lightly browned. When taken out of oven brush tops with 2 tbl. more of melted butter.

MS. PEGGY'S BIG BATCH O' BISCUITS
Recipe by Peggy Brown

I was talking with the wonderful Ms. Peggy Brown of Peggy's Heavenly Home Cooking soul food restaurant, bemoaning the fact that I cannot for the life of me make a great batch of biscuits. It is the one thing that still eludes me. She agreed with me that biscuits require a magic touch. "You gotta hold your mouth right when you make 'em," she told me her grandmother used to tell her. The ingredients are fairly simple: flour, shortening, buttermilk. But how you work the dough can make all the difference between brilliance and failure. Ms. Peggy insists that this is the best recipe for biscuits and she is adamant that you MUST use Martha White Self-Rising Flour and Crisco shortening. Nothing else will do. This recipe is for large batches of biscuits; it makes 2 dozen biscuits. I plan to cut the recipe in half and give it a try. You can give it a shot too. She also believes that the biscuits should be baked at a lower temperature than almost every other recipe I've ever seen. She says that if using a gas oven bake them at 375 degrees and if an electric oven at 400 degrees.

2 lbs. of Martha White Self-Rising Flour
1 qt. of buttermilk
1 heaping cup of Crisco shortening

Preparation:

In a very large mixing bowl add all the flour. Make a well in the middle of the flour and add the Crisco shortening. Add small amounts of buttermilk, working it into the flour and shortening with your fingers. Continue until you have worked in all the buttermilk. The dough should not be too wet nor too dry. According to Ms. Peggy it needs to be the consistency of Play-Doh. If it reaches this particular "feel" to your hands, do not attempt to pick up any flour left in bottom of bowl. Turn out dough onto a well-floured board. Ms. Peggy rolls out her dough with a rolling pin to about 1" thickness. Allow dough to rest about five minutes. Placing hands underneath dough, gently pull it up off the board and gingerly set it back onto board. She claims this helps settle the dough. Using a biscuit cutter, cut out your biscuits and place them touching one another in a cast iron skillet or cookie sheet. Bake at 375 degrees in a pre-heated oven (400 degrees if your oven is an electric one) until tops are brown.

MOM'S QUICK HOMEMADE ROLLS

½ package of yeast
¼ cup sugar
2 cups warm water
1 egg, beaten
¾ cup melted butter
4 cups self-rising flour

Preparation:

Pre-heat oven to 425 degrees. Dissolve yeast and sugar in warm water. Add beaten egg and mix well. In mixing bowl add melted butter in small measures alternating with small measures of flour; stir together well. Add yeast/sugar/water mixture slowly and blend well. You do not need to allow time for the dough to rise. Spoon dough into greased muffin tins. Bake until tops are golden brown. Dough may be refrigerated for up to a week.

SWEET TOOTH (DESSERTS)

MS. LARTHY'S CHOCOLATE POUND CAKE

For cake:
2 boxes Pillsbury Plus White cake mix
1 cup vegetable oil
2 cups water
6 whole eggs

For frosting:
2 cups confectioner's sugar; add more if needed
2 cups Hershey's chocolate powder; add more if needed
½ stick margarine
1 cup milk

Preparation:

Place all cake ingredients into a mixer and mix well for 20 minutes. Pour mixture into a pound cake pan. Bake for 1 hour and 15 minutes. Allow to cool and remove from pan.

Mix all frosting ingredients together in mixing bowl. Stir well until smoothly blended. Spread on cake. Cut and serve.

YOUR BASIC CHOCOLATE CAKE

1 box of Pillsbury Moist Supreme Classic Yellow Premium Cake Mix
1/3 stick of butter or margarine
1 cup water
3 eggs

Preparation:

Blend all ingredients together in an electric mixer for 15 minutes on normal/medium speed. Pour batter into two 9-inch baking pans. Bake for 30 minutes at 350 degrees. Let cool before adding frosting.

CHOCOLATE FROSTING FOR CAKE

1 cup Hershey's Powdered Chocolate to start; add more if needed
½ stick of margarine
3 cups of powdered sugar
¾ cup whole milk

Preparation:

Mix together in electric mixer for 5-10 minutes on slow speed. When thoroughly mixed and creamy, it is ready to add to cake.

7-UP CAKE

Note: a heavy-duty electric mixer is needed for this recipe

4 cups sugar
1 pd. butter
6 medium to large eggs
4 cups all-purpose flour
1 tsp. lemon extract
8 oz. of 7-Up or other similar soft drink

Preparation:

Blend sugar and butter together in electric mixer for 20 minutes. This step is very important in getting the cake texture just right. Add all eggs. Mix five minutes. Add flour. Mix ten minutes. Add lemon extract and 7-Up. Mix ten minutes. Pour batter into well-greased pound cake pan. Bake 1 hour 15 minutes at 350 degrees. Can be served warm or cold.

MY GRANNY'S "PINK LADY" STRAWBERRY CAKE
Recipe and Narrative by Jasmine Parks

Note: This recipe is from a former student of mine at LeMoyne-Owen College. Jasmine Parks wrote this recipe for a freshman composition assignment, a "process" or how-to essay. She wrote it in 2008 and I was impressed enough with both the narrative and the mouth-watering effect of the recipe that I kept it all this time since. I contacted Jasmine for permission to use the recipe in this book because it is such a good recipe and it follows the theme of this book about the importance of passing family recipes on to future generations. Jasmine was especially touched by my request for her Granny's recipe because since she wrote her essay in 2008 her Granny has passed on. As I've stated in this book, my own mother passed as I began this book. As I went through a box of my Mom's recipes after she was laid to rest, I came across a recipe for strawberry cake similar in many ways to this one.

– *Tom Graves*

Allison Graves Buchanan

Jasmine Parks:

Most families have a special recipe that is passed down from generation to generation. They have that special dish that is placed in the center of the table on important holidays. For my family, that recipe is my Granny's "Pink Lady" Strawberry Cake. Granny uses a variety of ingredients, techniques, and love to make her not-so-usual strawberry cake. With that in mind, allow me to enlighten you on how to make my Granny's special cake.

Granny is what our family calls an "individual cook." What that means is she cooks in her own way. These days many people buy a box of Duncan Hines cake mix, stir in some water, and call that a cake. Granny's Strawberry Cake is made totally from scratch. "Only the best will do and that only comes with work from you!" My Granny said those words and made them famous to everyone in our family.

So, to start off the best-ever strawberry cake, you need the following:

Ingredients for Granny's "Pink Lady" Strawberry Cake:

3 9-inch round cake pans
1¾ cups all-purpose flour
1 ½ tsp. baking powder
¾ cup milk
4 tbl. sifted cake flour
½ box Strawberry Jell-O
1 pkg (5-oz) frozen strawberries or equivalent fresh strawberries
½ cup of water and strawberry juice (from the strawberries)
1 cup canola oil
4 large eggs
1 ½ cups sugar plus one extra tbl.
1 tbl. vanilla extract
1 stick of butter cut into three equal pieces plus an additional 4 tbl. butter
¼ tsp. red food coloring to make the cake look pretty
one or two pinches of salt
several drops of LorAnn brand orange oils flavor or other orange flavoring
Note: You can make this cake in a single layer as shown in the photograph. Also, some of our taste testers thought adding a drizzle of icing or flavored glaze would make this cake even better

Preheat oven to 350 degrees. Cut up strawberries into thin slices. Place strawberries and one tbl. of sugar into medium mixing bowl. Mix together. The strawberries will make a sweet liquor in the bowl that later in the recipe will be combined with water to make ½ cup of liquid. While the strawberries are enjoying their bath, combine all-purpose flour, cake flour, baking powder, canola oil, eggs, strawberries, sugar, vanilla extract, sugar, Strawberry Jell-O, food coloring, 4 tbl. butter (melted), and milk.

Unfortunately, for those who are afraid of hard work, this cake will become your worst enemy at this point. Granny did not own a mixer. She stirred by hand. So if you want to do it Granny's way get those hands ready to stir, stir, and stir (about four minutes at least) some more until there are no lumps left in the mixture. After mixing by hand, fold in the water-and-strawberry juice liquor you have reserved. Stir well.

Next, cut up your stick of butter into three pieces of equal size. Place them in the waiting cake pans. Place those pans in the oven so the butter can melt.

Remove cake pans from oven and pour batter evenly into the three pans. The butter will help the cake form a nice crust. Bake for 30 minutes or until a toothpick comes out clean when inserted into the cakes. Allow cake to cool on a baking rack for 30 minutes. Stack the cakes one on top of each other and sprinkle a tablespoon of powdered sugar on top to make a lovely decoration. Some people like to sprinkle the powdered sugar using stencils, which look pretty and are artistic.

This cake is so good it doesn't need any icing. Some folks just can't do without adding some icing, and if I'm speaking to you then by all means add your favorite icing. But that's not Granny's way. All you need now is a fork (to sample the cake, dears) and a glass of water after all that hard work. Some of us are not as used to hard work as Granny.

NOT FROM SCRATCH BUT SO WHAT? STRAWBERRY CAKE

This recipe may not be the heirloom showpiece of the preceding strawberry cake recipe, but I guarantee you it is one of the most delicious cakes you will ever put in your mouth. One of the notions I've tried to steer clear of in this cookbook is that all great recipes MUST be made from scratch. That is a conceit foisted upon us by the uptown chefs of this world and the gourmands who believe that for those uptown prices their food had better not come out of a box. But in today's soul food kitchen, where the housewife is virtually a thing of the past, people on the run have to take advantage of the offerings at the corner grocery. Some highly creative soul food cooks such as Ms. Larthy have a kind of genius for finding the right combinations of store bought items to mix with fresh-from-the-farm foods.

For one of our cooking lessons, Ms. Larthy brought this strawberry cake. She sliced off a big chunk for me to take home with me (I eat sweets only one day per week since I am diabetic) and prepared slices for the church workers who can't get enough of her food. Later that week when I tried the cake I was in sweet tooth heaven. As I've explained, my Mom baked cakes and turned it into a small cottage business. My brother and I both got pretty sick of cakes and the sweet aromas of them in the oven. So it takes a lot for me to get worked up over a cake, but this one sure did it for me.

1 15.25-oz. box of Pillsbury Strawberry Cake Mix
1 cup water
½ cup vegetable oil
3 eggs

Preparation:

Using a mixer, blend all ingredients together on medium speed for five minutes. Pour batter into two 9-inch round pans and bake for 29-33 minutes at 350 degrees.

Frosting: Use the pre-made Pillsbury Creamy Supreme Strawberry Frosting.

FRESH APPLE CAKE

1 medium apple
1 ½ cups chopped walnuts
2 cups sugar
2 cups flour
1 tsp. nutmeg
1 tsp. cinnamon
2 eggs
1 stick melted margarine

Preparation:

Peel and core apple and cut into very small bite-sized pieces. Stirring well, mix all ingredients together in mixing bowl. Pour into a 9" x 13" baking pan and bake for 35 minutes at 350 degrees. Let cool and cut into squares.

MS. LARTHY'S CLASSIC KARO PECAN PIE

3 eggs
1 cup sugar
1 cup dark Karo syrup
2 tbl. melted margarine
1 ½ cups pecans
1 tsp. vanilla extract
9" frozen pie shell

Preparation:

Beat eggs well in mixing bowl. Add all other ingredients (except pecans) and mix well. Pour into pie shell. Add layer of pecans on top of pie filling. Bake in 350 degree oven for 60 minutes. Let cool. Serve.

MY MOM'S KARO PECAN PIE VARIATION

My Mom was known for her pecan pie. This is her long-time recipe, which is a slight variation on Ms. Larthy's recipe above.

3 eggs
½ cup sugar
1 cup "red label" white Karo syrup
1/8 tsp. salt
1 tbl. butter
1 cup pecans
9" frozen pie shell

Preparation:

Beat eggs well in mixing bowl. Add all other ingredients (except pecans) and mix well. Pour into pie shell. Add layer of pecans on top of pie filling. Bake in 325 degree oven for 60 minutes. If not completely done, add 10 more minutes of baking time.

YVONNE MITCHELL'S BOURBON PECAN PIE
Recipe by Yvonne Mitchell

9" inch deep dish pie shell
1 cup light brown sugar packed down
2 large eggs
½ cup butter melted (one stick)
2 tbl. of milk
1 tbl. of self-rising flour
1 ½ tbl. of vanilla extract
1 cup of pecan halves
¼ cup of pecan pieces
2 shots of (Four Roses Single Barrel) bourbon

Preparation:

1. Mix sugar, butter and eggs and milk, flour, vanilla extract, and bourbon.
2. Fold in ¼ cup of pecan pieces and pour into pie shell.

3. Arrange 1 cup pecan halves on top of pie.
4. Bake at 325° for 45 minutes until nice and done.

OLD FASHIONED APPLE PIE

5 medium apples peeled and cut into small pieces
2 cups sugar
1 tsp. nutmeg
1 stick margarine
1 9" frozen pie shell
1 can Pillsbury biscuits

Preparation:

Cook apple pieces in water to cover for one hour until apples are very soft. Pour off water and put apples in mixing bowl. Add sugar, nutmeg, and melted margarine to apples and mix well. Pour mixture into pie shell. Take biscuit dough and roll it with roller until thin and elongated. Cut elongated biscuit dough into strips that are placed in a cross-hatch fashion on top of pie.

Bake at 350 degrees for one hour until crust and topping are nice and brown. Allow to cool slightly and serve. Delicious with ice cream!

LEMON ICE BOX PIE

3 large eggs
2 14-oz. cans of sweetened condensed milk
1 cup concentrated lemon juice
1 10-inch graham cracker pie crust
whipped cream
1 cup graham cracker crumbs, finely ground

Preparation:

Break and separate three eggs. Beat egg yolks well. Add condensed milk. Stir until batter is smooth. Add 1 cup of concentrated lemon juice . Stir again until smooth. Pour mixture into 10-inch graham cracker pie crust. Chill for at least eight hours. Top with whipped cream. Sprinkle with a dusting of graham cracker crumbs.

HELPFUL HINT: To firm up the filling we suggest you put the pie in the freezer. Otherwise the pie can be a little runny. Delicious, but runny. In the freezer the pie, of course, will harden. We suggest you carefully slice the pie for the servings you need and leave each serving out for around 30 minutes. The filling should be at the perfect consistency after 30 minutes.

MS. LARTHY'S FRIED PEACH PIE

2 16-oz. packages dried peaches
1 ½ cups sugar
1 stick margarine
½ tsp. nutmeg
½ tsp. vanilla extract
1 can Pillsbury biscuits

Preparation:

In small pan, cover peaches with water and cook about one hour over medium-low heat until peaches are very soft and tender. Add water during cooking if needed. Drain off water and mash peaches until pulpy. Add sugar, margarine, nutmeg, and vanilla. Stir together well. Pillsbury biscuits will be used as the crust for the fried pie. Roll out dough until quite thin. Cut a circle out of dough—you can cut around a cereal bowl for a good and appropriate shape. Place a scoop of peach filling in the middle of your circle of dough and spread. Fold circle of dough in half and pinch together edges; filling should be completely contained within your dough pocket without dripping from any opening. Fry in oil that covers pie only about halfway. When fry side is properly browned, flip pie over and brown the other side. Serve immediately when done.

MS. LARTHY'S OLD FASHIONED PEACH COBBLER

1 29-oz. can peaches
1 ½ cups sugar
1 stick margarine
½ tsp. nutmeg
½ tsp. vanilla extract
1 can Pillsbury biscuits
9" frozen pie shell

As in the fried pie recipe in this book, cover peaches with water in an appropriate-sized pot and cook about one hour over medium-low heat until peaches are very soft and tender and the juice thickens. Add water during cooking if necessary. Add sugar, margarine, nutmeg, and vanilla. Stir together well. Pillsbury biscuits will be used as the crust topping. Roll out dough until thin. Add peach mixture to pie shell. Place dough on top of peach mixture until covered and cut off any dough that hangs over edge of pie pan. Cook until dough topping is nice and brown. Serve with ice cream.

SWEET POTATO PIE

3 medium sweet potatoes
2 eggs
¾ stick of margarine
1 cup sugar
1 tsp. vanilla extract
½ tsp. nutmeg
½ cup Carnation Evaporated Milk
9" frozen pie shell

Preparation:

Peel potatoes and slice into ¼" rounds. Cook in water until very soft. Drain. Put in electric mixer, add eggs, margarine, and all other ingredients. Mix well for at least 5-10 minutes until totally smooth. Pour into pie shell. Bake 1 ½ hours at 350 degrees until done. Let cool. Add Cool Whip if you like. Serve.

MS. LARTHY'S BETTER THAN SCRATCH BANANA PUDDING

Tom Graves

This is one of Ms. Larthy's masterpieces. The secret is the blending of the Concord brand filling with the Jell-O instant pudding mix, which makes an almost perfect consistency. The Concord filling is available only at certain grocery chains (Save-A-Lot) and on Amazon.com. You may have to hunt it down, but it will ultimately be worth it.

1 3.4-oz. box Jell-O Banana Cream Instant Pudding Mix
1 16-oz. pouch Concord Banana Creme Flavored Pudding & Pie Filling
1 14-oz. can condensed milk
1 ½ bags vanilla wafers (Note: I used a single one-pound bag)
1 ½ tubs whipped cream (in tub, not spray can) or Cool Whip
5 ripe bananas
½ cup graham cracker crumbs grated fine

Preparation:

Line a 14" x 10" x 2" (or close) pan with vanilla wafers. Blend Jell-O Pudding Mix (just the powder from the package) with Concord Banana Creme Flavored Pudding & Pie Filling and condensed milk. Stir well. Spread mix over vanilla wafers, smoothing with a spoon. Cut bananas into ¼" thick slices and layer on top of the pudding mix until covered with a single layer. Top with layer of whipped cream or Cool Whip. Do not use a spray can as I did, because the spray can will not cover the full pan of banana pudding. You will have to do like me and go back to the store for more. Sprinkle top of whipped cream with a good dusting of graham cracker crumbs. Chill well in refrigerator and serve.

The secret ingredient to Ms. Larthy's superb banana pudding.

MOM'S PEANUT BUTTER COOKIES

1 cup sugar
2 eggs
2 tsp. baking soda
½ cup butter
1 tsp. vanilla extract
1 cup brown sugar
1 cup creamy peanut butter
3 cups flour

Preparation:

Cream sugar and butter together. Add well-beaten eggs. Stir in peanut butter. Add flour and baking soda sifted together. Add vanilla extract. Refrigerate dough for one hour. Pinch small balls from the dough and form into cookies. Shape with fork and using fork make a criss-cross pattern on the top of cookie. This makes them taste better.

Preheat oven to 375 degrees. Bake for 10 minutes or until done.

MOM'S LADY FINGERS

Lots of cookies, pastries, and British-type biscuits are called lady fingers. My Mom called these cookies both lady fingers and butter fingers. These were made for fancy hosting, when the ladies were over for a tea. They invariably produced some oohs and aahs when served.

2 ¼ cups all-purpose flour
¾ cup powdered sugar
2 sticks butter
1 tsp. vanilla extract
1 cup chopped pecans

Preparation:

Melt butter. Mix all ingredients except sugar in mixing bowl and form a dough. Pinch off small balls of dough and form into a finger shape. Bake lady fingers at 350 degrees for 20 to 30 minutes. Roll in powdered sugar when done baking. Serve.

WHISTLE WETTERS (BEVERAGES)

AUNT MERLE'S SECRET SWEET TEA

Sweet tea, "the table wine of the Deep South," is yet another one of those deceptively simple recipes of which there must be a thousand ways to royally foul up. You may be thinking that there is no way to ruin something as simple as brewing tea bags in hot water. My Mom, may she rest in perfect peace, never ever could get sweet tea to taste like anything that couldn't be skated on. Her tea was forever cloudy, bitter, and just barely drinkable. She did not use tea bags at all but instead the archaic loose leaf tea that only she seemed to use. Mom never measured either the tea or the water. She dumped it in a pot, turned on the faucet, and what wound up in the tea pitcher that evening is whatever voodoo brew happened to boil up on the stove.

Imagine then my surprise at the wonder brew my Aunt Merle Graves served at her table…clear, robust, sweet, and as close to a table wine as any non-alcoholic beverage I've had the pleasure to imbibe. What was her secret? How was her sweet tea always so dead perfect?

I put this question to her son, my cousin Rick, and he confirmed that Aunt Merle's tea was known wide and far in her city in Arkansas. He thinks it may have had something to do with the particularly sweet and good water in Pine Bluff. Memphis, where I live, has some of the world's highest rated water, but I agree that Pine Bluff's was just as good. Another secret is that she immediately refrigerated the tea after brewing. She believed that chilling the tea added to its flavor and allowed the sugar to blend well. See if you agree.

4 tea bags (Lipton brand)
10 cups water, total
sugar to taste

Preparation:

In a small pot put 4 tea bags in 4 cups of water. Bring to a boil and let boil about three minutes. Turn off heat, cover, and allow to steep for about 15 minutes. Remove tea bags, add desired sugar (Southerners like it sweet enough for your dentist to make a house call), add roughly six more cups of cool water (less if you like strong tea), mix well, and immediately refrigerate. When well-chilled serve over ice.
Note: In several Hollywood films set in the South I've watched tea being served without ice in the glasses. In my life I have never once seen anyone serve tea that was not over ice. Not once. Not even in the dead of winter. How this silly and inaccurate trope got started in movies, I haven't a clue. But it needs to stop. Francis Ford Coppola, are you paying attention?

MS. LARTHY'S SPECIAL PARTY TEA

During our very first cooking lesson Ms. Larthy introduced me to her Special Party Tea. I do not much like instant tea, any more than I like instant coffee. But one must make exceptions when the end product is this good. Lipton's Peach flavor instant tea is pretty much available everywhere in the U.S., but it's a bit harder to find the Orange Mango Tang. Ms. Larthy informed me that she gets hers at Wal-Mart. If you find the Mango Tang impossible to get, just substitute the original Orange Tang, which is available everywhere. I'm not sure how she stumbled onto this shoutingly good combination of flavors, but after one sip I was hooked. She now makes me some almost every cooking lesson and although I only eat sugar on Friday—my doctor allows me only one sugar day a week due to me having Type 2 diabetes as of a couple of years ago—I have been forced to make exception after exception due to this wonderful drink.

1 cup Lipton's Peach Iced Tea Mix
½ cup Orange Mango Tang (available at Wal-Marts)
8 cups water
½ cup sugar

Preparation:

Blend all ingredients together in tall pitcher. Chill. Serve over ice.

TRADITIONAL ETHIOPIAN HOT TEA WITH MILK

My ex-wife, Bintou Ndiaye, and I have remained good friends since going our separate ways and on occasion still meet for dinner to catch up on each other's lives and have a good laugh or two. Although she was born in Sierra Leone and later lived in Senegal, her father's home country, she still had a great curiosity for African food from other regions. About a decade ago we decided to try a new Ethiopian restaurant in town and were both excited by the exotic new tastes brought to our table. Since then, there have been several other Ethiopian restaurants to open in Memphis. A smaller, homey restaurant, Derae, introduced me to the best hot tea I've had in my life. On occasion I would stop there and order a large hot tea to take with me.

I became curious about this superb hot drink from Ethiopia and began to research it. I found several recipes on-line and refined the better ones into the one you see here. I brought some for Ms. Larthy to try and after taking a few sips she said, "Whoo! This is the captain of teas!"

Needed: Tea kettle (mine is a stove top whistling model)

4-5 Lipton tea bags
10 whole cloves
6 whole cardamom seeds
1 cinnamon stick
10 cups water
sugar to taste
milk to taste, heated

Preparation:

Add water, then all ingredients except sugar and milk to kettle. Bring to a boil. Let sit for five minutes. Remove tea bags and strain through a strainer. Pour into cups and add desired sugar while hot and heated milk to taste. Wonderful on cold, wintry nights!

PUNCH IT UP FRUIT PUNCH

1 package no sugar Strawberry Kool-Aid
1 package no sugar Tropical Punch Kool-Aid
1 package no sugar Orange Kool-Aid
1 package no sugar Peach Mango Kool-Aid
1 cup orange juice
2 cups of 7-Up or Sprite or ginger ale
sugar to taste
water to taste

Preparation:

Add all ingredients together in a large pitcher. Add sugar as desired and water to desired strength as well (some folks like their punch lighter and more watered-down, and some folks like less water and stronger flavor). Pour over ice.

DON'T FAIL ME FRUIT SMOOTHIE

Smoothies, of course, are a fad thing. Smoothie franchises did not exist a generation ago, at least not in Memphis. But they are most certainly a welcome attraction and substitute well for a dessert, particularly to those of us who must restrict our sugar intake. This recipe is simple, a family favorite, and you simply can't go wrong with it. Pineapple, strawberries, and banana marry wonderfully as flavors.

1 ripe banana
1 cup frozen strawberries
1 cup frozen pineapple pieces
1 cup whole milk
1 six-oz. container of vanilla yogurt

Preparation:

Put all ingredients together in a heavy-duty blender. Blend well. Serve immediately. It tastes better if you drink it through two straws rather than one.

AUTHENTIC AFRICAN GINGER BEER
Recipe by Bintou Ndiaye

Tom Graves

Ginger beer is different things to different people. In some countries it is fermented and contains alcohol, in others it is a carbonated soft drink, and in many cultures the ginger root goes through a laborious process before the drink is made. This recipe is how ginger beer is made in West Africa and my former wife, Bintou Ndiaye, makes the Sierra Leonian version which is much in demand among her Sierra Leonian friends here in the U.S. Whenever there is a major social event she is begged to make her ginger beer and you can see people contentedly sipping their drinks until the beverage, as always, runs out. Please note that this ginger beer is both sweet and spicy hot, a curious blend of the two.

3 pods of fresh ginger root
¼ cup sweetened vanilla syrup
2 cups sugar

Preparation:

Peel covering off ginger root pods the same as if they were potatoes you were peeling. Chop pods into thick pieces and place into a very heavy duty blender with 2 cups of water. Blend for one to two minutes until ginger is liquefied into a fine pulp. Using a large kitchen strainer pour ginger root pulp into strainer and let juice drain into a large bowl. Put remaining pulp in strainer back into blender and add 4 more cups of water. Blend well for at least one minute. Strain well through strainer getting all juice out of pulp that is possible.

Add vanilla syrup and sugar to juice. Stir well and refrigerate. Serve over ice.

THE ERNEST HEMINGWAY
ORIGINAL EL FLORIDITA DAIQUIRI

Tom Graves

One of my biggest regrets in life, and one that I cannot fully explain, even to myself, is that I haven't traveled abroad more. That said, I admit that the places I have traveled were rapturously exotic and filled with curiosities and intrigue. About eight years ago, at the urging of a physician friend, I dashed off to Havana, Cuba and spent an unforgettable week in the real, unvarnished Fidel Castro Cuba. I loved it. I have so many stories to tell from that adventure that I'd better stop right there and get onto the subject at hand: the mixing of one of the great drinks of the mid-Twentieth Century, the daiquiri, now ubiquitous in bars around the nation, and about as bastardized in those bars as a drink could get. A green apple daiquiri? No problem. Here you go.

But what I discovered in Havana was the El Floridita bar, Ernest Hemingway's old hangout. That's where he was given a concoction that he in turn rhapsodized to the whole world. When you go to El Floridita today, you are met with a bronze statue of old man Hemingway over in the corner and busloads of tourists from every corner of the globe there for a taste of Hemingway to tell the folks about back home.

Ms. Larthy, by the way, does not drink. However, we both agreed that there wasn't any reason not to share a few good cocktail recipes. There is nothing like this daiquiri when sitting comfortably outdoors with friends. No one seems to be quite in absolute agreement on the exact measurements of the ingredients, but this is the recipe I use with great success. The secret of the taste of the real authentic Cuban daiquiri is the Luxardo maraschino liqueur. Try it. You'll like it.

1 ½-oz. light rum (Havana Club if you can get it)
½-oz. fresh-squeezed lime juice
¼-oz. simple syrup
¼-oz. Luxardo maraschino liqueur

Preparation:

Add all ingredients to a cocktail shaker filled with ice. Shake well. Pour into a chilled daiquiri glass.

Tom Graves

SINGAPORE SLING

One of my favorite writers, Charles Willeford, once wrote that the Singapore Sling was the most delicious drink in the world. I cannot find fault with this statement. Memphis voted in liquor-by-the-drink right when I turned 18, which coincided with the lowering of drinking age from 21 to 18. As you might imagine, flocks of young people crowded the new bars that sprang up overnight. One of the popular drinks was the Singapore Sling, perfect for kids like us who hadn't yet developed tastes for hard liquor.

For reasons I don't know, the Sling's popularity did not last. I've ordered it in bars where the bartender had to look it up in a book. Tiki bars and tiki drinks have become very retro these days, and the Singapore Sling has assumed its rightful place as the drink of drinks.

I can't think of a better beverage to add a little umbrella to.

1-oz. gin
2-oz. sour mix
½ - ¾-oz. grenadine
a dash of cherry brandy
club soda

Pour gin, sour mix, and grenadine into a cocktail shaker filled with ice. Shake well. Pour into tall cocktail glass filled with ice. Add about ½ oz. of club soda and then float a dash of cherry brandy on top.
Note: experiment with the amount of club soda you prefer. Too much will water down the flavors.

SIDE ATTRACTIONS

MS. LARTHY'S WORK OF ART MACARONI AND CHEESE

16-oz. box of macaroni
2 tbl. salt
1 tsp. pepper
3 eggs
1 cup evaporated milk
2 cups Ragu Double Cheddar Cheese sauce
1 stick oleo margarine, melted
1 cup shredded mild cheddar cheese plus one extra handful
½ tsp. yellow food coloring

Preparation:

Pour dry macaroni into suitable pot and cover with cool tap water. Add 1 tbl. salt. Cook over low flame for 20 to 30 minutes stirring occasionally. Macaroni should be well-done by this time. Drain off hot water and cover with cool water. Let sit for 10 minutes so that macaroni is cooled.

Pour off water.

In a mixing bowl stir in three eggs. Beat well. Stir in 1 cup of evaporated milk. Stir in 1 cup of Ragu cheese sauce. Stir mixture well. Add 1 tbl. salt and tsp. pepper. Add 1 cup of shredded cheddar cheese and melted stick of margarine. Stir well. Add yellow food coloring. Stir all together until well mixed.

Pour all ingredients over macaroni. Mix very well. Pour into appropriately-sized pan. Smooth mixture until level. Sprinkle handful of shredded cheddar on top. Pour remaining cup of Ragu cheese sauce on top and smooth out until topping is nice and pretty.

Place in a pre-heated 350 degree oven. Bake for 40-45 minutes until top of mixture is just beginning to crust.

Remove from oven and allow to sit five minutes. Serve while still hot and gooey.

ETHAN'S MAC AND CHEESE
Recipe by Yvonne Mitchell

Yvonne Mitchell, affectionately known as Aunt Von by her family, is the daughter of famed record producer and recording artist Willie Mitchell, now deceased, who brought Al Green, Ann Peeples, and many other soul luminaries to the world. Mr. Mitchell owned Royal Studios in South Memphis, which is still in operation. Ms. Yvonne Mitchell was a surprise benefit for those recording at Royal Studios because she cooked soul food dinners for everyone. No one left hungry or without shouting praises for her food. Through the grapevine in Memphis it was known to sit at her table and eat her food if ever you can. She has given me permission to use two of her recipes for this book: this macaroni and cheese recipe named after a friend and her much-applauded Bourbon Pecan Pie.

2 cups of elbow macaroni
1 tbl. of salt
1 tbl. of olive oil
12-oz. can of evaporated milk
3 large eggs
7 tbl. of butter
1½ cup of finely shredded Mexican cheese
2 cups of finely shredded sharp cheddar cheese
½ teaspoon of ground mustard

Preparation:

1. Preheat oven 400°
2. Boil 10 cups of water in medium to large size pot. Add salt and olive oil to the water on medium high heat. Add macaroni when water comes to a boil. Boil 10 to 15 minutes.
3. Get a medium size bowl and mix the eggs with a whisk. Add in ground mustard; gradually mix in evaporated milk. Mix well.
4. Take a large mixing bowl. Add noodles, seven tablespoons of butter and add all cheese except a ½ cup of sharp finely shredded cheese which is added to top.
5. Pour mixture in a 9"x11" casserole dish, add ½ cup of sharp cheddar cheese to top, cover with the cover of your baking dish or aluminum foil. Bake on 400° for 20-25 minutes. Remove from oven and let set for 5 minutes. Enjoy.

MS. LARTHY'S HANDMADE SPAGHETTI AND MEATBALLS

One of the more curious developments in the long history of soul food cuisine is the adaptation of the staple Italian dish of spaghetti and meatballs. I am not aware of any soul food restaurant that does not have spaghetti as a side item. The tomato sauce is typically a little more peppery than the Italian version, and some cooks prepare meatballs while others prefer meat sauce. Either version is good to me. Ms. Larthy, as you have surely noticed while reading this book, does not always prepare things from scratch. Here she uses Hunt's spaghetti sauce straight off the grocery store shelf.

My wonderful mother-in-law from my first marriage, the late Lucille Maimone, used an old family recipe for her spaghetti and meatballs that had been passed down from her husband's grandmother direct from Sicily. Oh how I miss those Sundays when she would cook a huge meal for us of her spaghetti and meatballs. The recipe is a family secret and will be passed down exclusively to her heirs.

As good as that recipe is, my favorite made-from-scratch spaghetti and meatballs can be found in *The Scorsese Family Cookbook* from film director Martin Scorsese's mother, Catherine Scorsese. It is labor intensive, but one taste will make you think you are in a Sicilian kitchen preparing for a holiday feast.

1 lb. ground beef
¾ cup of chopped bell pepper, celery, and onion combined
salt
pepper
Italian seasoning powder
1 jar of Hunt's spaghetti sauce or your favorite tomato sauce
1 package spaghetti

Preparation:

Season ground beef liberally with salt, pepper, and Italian seasoning powder. Add chopped ingredients. Roll meatballs to desired size. Brown meatballs in skillet with a tablespoon or so of vegetable oil. When browned, drain oil and add tomato sauce. Cook spaghetti separately to desired level of doneness (Italians like spaghetti cooked "al dente" which translated means "to the tooth" or with a slight crunch still left in the noodle. Most soul food cooks like their spaghetti thoroughly cooked.) When spaghetti is done, drain water and mix in meatballs and sauce. Serve.

MS. LARTHY'S LASAGNA

Memphis had a large influx of Southern Italian and Sicilian immigrants in the early 20th Century. Throughout the city small mom and pop restaurants blossomed that served basic Southern Italian fare such as spaghetti and meatballs, ravioli, and lasagna. Because this food was inexpensive, many African Americans patronized these establishments, some dining in in segregated sections of the restaurant, many more ordering take-out. Italian food became a staple for black Memphians and enterprising cooks learned to make these dishes, applying their own curious soul food twists to the recipes. My first wife was from just such an Italian background and I have eaten the best of the best of this cuisine. My former sister-in-law, Diane Scott, makes a Christmas lasagna that is the prize dish of the season. But Ms. Larthy's lasagna recipe comes mighty close in deliciousity.

2 pds. ground beef
1 6-oz. can tomato paste
1 can or jar of spaghetti sauce (your desired brand)
1 8-oz. package of mozzarella cheese
1 8-oz. package of cheddar cheese
1 tbl. Italian seasoning
1 tsp. black pepper
1 pinch of red pepper
½ cup chopped onion
½ cup chopped green pepper
½ cup chopped celery
1 package lasagna noodles
3 cups water

Preparation:

Brown ground beef in skillet or pot. Separately, cook lasagna noodles according to directions on package. When ground beef is browned, add tomato paste, spaghetti sauce, vegetables, and seasonings. When thoroughly mixed, add 3 cups of water and allow to simmer for 10 minutes. In a baking pan of your choice, add a layer of the meat mixture. Over that add a layer of lasagna noodles. Then add a layer of cheddar cheese topped with another layer of meat, another layer of lasagna noodles, then another layer of cheddar cheese. Top with a final layer of mozzarella cheese. Bake in oven for 30 minutes at 350 degrees. Cool slightly and serve.

THE ONLY GOOD HOMEMADE PIZZA
Recipe by James Newcomb

Jim Newcomb is one of my oldest friends and mentored me as a budding writer while I was an undergraduate at the University of Memphis. He was my freshman English teacher and is the first person to ever tell me I might have a talent for writing. I owe him much.

About the time I turned 40 I returned to the university to earn my M.F.A. in Creative Writing. The English Department at the U of M has a renowned writers' lecture series that brings in notable authors and poets. After the lecture or reading, the faculty and students typically fete the author or poet at the home of a faculty member and some of these get-togethers afterward are more memorable than the lectures. (For example, I will never forget the night I sat next to Susan Orlean, chowing down on ribs from The Rendezvous restaurant, and talking in detail about the all-sister rock and roll group The Shaggs.) Ishmael Reed, the famed African American author of *Mumbo Jumbo* and *The Last Days of Louisiana Red*, was the honored guest one semester and the after-party was to be held at the lovely Midtown home of my mentor Jim Newcomb. Jim is a very good cook and for this occasion he prepared his studiously concocted homemade pizza. The aroma of the pizza as it baked drew me into the kitchen and sitting at a kitchen table, waiting for the first pizza was Ishmael Reed. I sat across from him and we made small talk until Jim took the pizza out of the oven, cut it into slices, and gave us the first tastes. Reed and I wolfed our slices down as the second pizza went into the oven. Although we shared with the others at the reception, Reed and I pretty much hogged those pizzas and neither of us cared what the others thought. We both agreed that this was just about the finest homemade pizza we'd ever had.

I haven't crossed paths again with Ishmael Reed, but I learned that he left an interesting inscription in his book *Airing Dirty Laundry* for Jim that night. Here is what he wrote:

to
Jim--
All of the great pizza--all
Day you worked
on--
Ishmael Reed
Oct 27 '95

We must applaud Jim Newcomb for sharing his recipe for this book. This recipe is a bit more complicated than most recipes in this book, but as I got this recipe from Jim many years ago and have prepared it many times since, I can tell you it is actually not that hard to make. And the results are pretty spectacular.

Pizza dough

1 2/3 cups flour
1/3 cup whole wheat flour
1 tsp. salt
1 tbl. yeast
¾ cup of warm water
1 tsp. of sugar (or honey)
1 ½ tsp. of olive oil

Preparation:

Using a sifter, sift the two flours and salt together in a mixing bowl. Add yeast to warm water and stir vigorously to fully dissolve yeast. Add sugar (or honey) and again stir vigorously to dissolve. Set aside for three minutes, then add olive oil and stir vigorously. Add this yeast mixture to flour mixture in bowl. Mix with a fork or wooden spoon until dough hangs together. Knead in the bowl for three to five minutes adding sprinkling of flour as required to keep dough from sticking to the hands. Form into a dough ball and set bowl covered with a towel in a nice, warm place for the dough to rise, from 45 minutes to an hour.

Pizza makings

½ pd. of Italian or pork sausage cooked and then crumbled. You may substitute thinly sliced pepperoni
½ of small can of tomato sauce with herb seasonings already added
¼ pd. of thinly sliced mushrooms (optional)
½ package of frozen spinach, thawed
6 oz. of mozzarella cheese in block form. You may substitute mozzarella pre-shredded in package.
Parmesan cheese
Onion, chopped green pepper, minced garlic (optional)

Preparation:

Preheat oven to 390 degrees. Shred block of mozzarella cheese in a Cuisinart (or similar) food processor using grating blade. This produces a very fine angel hair-like shred that melts and bakes quickly while allowing steam from ingredients below it to escape. Lightly grease a 9" x 14" pan. Spread dough in pan and allow it to roll out on sides of pan with a bit of a ridge at the edges. Do not use a roller to roll out dough. Just finesse it into pan using your fingers. Spread a thin layer of the herbed tomato sauce on dough. Sprinkle bits of spinach over the whole bed of the pizza. Add a layer of mozzarella cheese over the whole thing. Add toppings as desired. Sprinkle a liberal layer of Parmesan cheese on top. Bake for 15 to 20 minutes until higher parts are a golden brown. Allow to rest for two or three minutes before cutting into slices. Serve.

MS. LARTHY'S BROCCOLI ALFREDO WITH HICKORY SMOKED SAUSAGE

1 12-oz. package of fettucine pasta
1 jar of Ragu Classic Alfredo Sauce
4 cups of chopped broccoli
1 ½ pounds of a good hickory smoked sausage sliced thin
½ cup shredded cheddar cheese

Preparation:

Cook pasta according to package directions. Drain. Steam the chopped broccoli. Add pasta, broccoli, Alfredo sauce, and sausage together in mixing bowl and mix well. Put ingredients in baking pan and add shredded cheese to top. Bake in 350 degree oven for 10 minutes and serve.

MS. LARTHY'S SUNDAY SOCIAL POTATO SALAD

5 medium red potatoes
4 eggs
1 tsp. salt
1 tbl. mustard
½ tsp. black pepper
½ sweet relish
½ cup green bell pepper
½ cup red bell pepper
½ cup celery, chopped
1 ½ cups mayonnaise
½ tsp. yellow food coloring

Preparation:

Peel potatoes and cut into small squares, about the size of a sugar cube. Cook potatoes until soft in water to cover with salt. Let cool then drain. Boil 4 eggs. Let cool. Grate the eggs into the potatoes you have set aside. Add all other ingredients and mix well. The food coloring and the different colors of the bell peppers make this dish look as good as it tastes. Refrigerate. Serve when cold. Makes about 8 servings.

THE AMERICAN GRILLED CHEESE SANDWICH

Is there any better food combination than soup and sandwich? Cold days are just made for a grilled cheese sandwich with a side of flavorful, warming hot soup. Grilled cheese sandwiches are so ridiculously easy to make that I hesitate to put an actual recipe in this book. However, what my generation takes for granted, new generations may not know at all. My maternal grandmother, a terrific cook, passed away when I was but 14 years old. And she took her recipe for outstanding biscuits with her. For reasons known only to my Mom, she refused to ask for or learn my grandmother's recipe, even though my brother and I begged her. So, here and now we will make sure our descendants can at least make a good ol' American grilled cheese sandwich. Note: I am told by reliable sources that if you order a grilled cheese in a fine restaurant, the chefs often add a layer of mayonnaise to the sandwich to give it a richer flavor. Although I prefer the basic recipe, experiment if you like.

2 slices of bread, white or wheat
2 slices of American cheese
2 pats of butter

Preparation:

Put 2 slices of cheese between the two slices of bread. In a thick skillet such as cast iron, melt one pat of butter over medium heat. When melted, place one side of sandwich into melted butter. Move the sandwich around with your hand to make sure the butter spreads well onto the bread. Keeping a close watch on the bottom of the sandwich, cook until bread is toasted to your desired brownness. With a spatula lift sandwich off skillet. Place second pat of butter on skillet and allow to melt, which it will do very quickly. Flip over sandwich, and toast the other side. Note that the skillet is pretty hot by now and the second side will toast much quicker than the first side. Keep an eye on it and take off skillet when done. Serve quickly while cheese is lovingly melted and creamy. Yum!

BAKED BEAN SUPER SIDE DISH

2 28-oz. cans of Bush's or other baked beans
1 cup of browned ground beef
½ cup chopped onions
1 tbl. butter
1 cup catsup

Preparation:

Saute onions in butter until soft and add ground beef and catsup. Mix in baked beans and stir well. Simmer for 10 minutes. Ready to serve hot.

COLE SLAW

1 cabbage finely grated (4 to 5 cups)
2 tsp. sugar
1 tsp. mustard
1 tsp. powdered cole slaw mix (Concord brand is what Ms. Larthy uses)
3 tbl. sweet relish
5 tbl. mayonnaise
2 tbl. diced white onion

Preparation:

Put all ingredients in a large mixing bowl. Mix thoroughly.

*Note: I am not much of a slaw man. Typically I don't even put slaw on my Memphis barbecue sandwiches. However, if the slaw is really good, I will ask for a side order and dab it on my barbecue or eat in small bites along with fried fish. Ms. Larthy's slaw here is highly flavored and very fresh out-of-the-garden tasting. It dances wonderfully with her fried catfish. Try them together.

MO CARLSON'S FANDIBULOUS TOMATO DRESSING

The late Mo Carlson was the wife of one of my great friends, the late writer Tom Carlson. She was a wonderful, fine lady from one of Minnesota's better families. We were all at a social event during the middle of tomato season and Mo brought sliced heirloom tomatoes with this fantastic marinade. I instantly asked—well, I begged a little—if she would give me her recipe and she kindly obliged.

Homegrown tomatoes (creole tomatoes are particularly good)
one red onion
fresh basil

Dressing ingredients:
1/4 cup double virgin olive oil
1/4 cup of vinegar
1/4 heaping tsp. cracked black pepper
1/4 heaping tsp. kosher salt
1/2 tsp. minced garlic
pinch of dry mustard powder

Preparation:

Slice tomatoes and place on a large plate. Chop onion into coarse bits and place over slices of tomato. Shred basil and put over tomatoes and onions. Ladle dressing over all tomato slices. Cover and chill for an hour.

MOM'S SHISH KABOB MARINADE

My mom developed and refined this recipe over several decades and it was a family favorite. Perfect for shish kabobs and, I'm sure, other grilled meats as well.

½ cup soy sauce
½ cup pineapple juice
¼ cup cooking oil
tsp. dry mustard
tbl. brown sugar
2 tsp. ground ginger
tsp. garlic salt
¼ tsp. fresh pepper

Preparation:

Simmer all ingredients in sauce pan at least 5 minutes. Let cool. Allow shish kabob meats to marinate in the ingredients one hour in refrigerator. While grilling, liberally brush shish kabobs with marinade.

TOM GRAVES' EXQUISITE BAY LEAF BARBECUE TABLE SAUCE

Like many Memphians I am a barbecue fanatic. I have friends who blog and write professionally about Memphis barbecue, which is hands-down the best in the world. We trade barbecue secrets like baseball fans trade prized bubblegum cards. A long-gone barbecue joint—one of the more eccentric ones at that—was Lamb's located in the heart of Midtown. Mr. Lamb, the owner, looked as if he stepped out of one of those Hobbit movies. Patrons were often startled when seated at the lunch counter and Mr. Lamb would come rolling out from under the other side of the counter, where he often napped hidden from view of the customers. He spent much of the night tending his barbecue. Such is the devotion in Memphis.

Lamb's had a thick table sauce unlike any I've tasted anywhere else. Very tangy, mildly hot, seasonings that really know how to work with smoked pork. By hook and crook and lots of experimentation, I've perfected a recipe that I think is very close to Lamb's. Again, please note this is a table sauce, not a basting sauce. It is meant to put on finished barbecue just prior to eating it.

1 can of Campbell's tomato soup
2 tbl. dry mustard

½ cup vegetable oil
2 or 3 crumbled bay leaves
½ tsp. red pepper
2 tbl. salt
1 small bottle Lea & Perrins Worcestershire sauce
1 tsp. black pepper
1 cup vinegar

Preparation:

Mix all ingredients in a sauce pan except the vinegar. Bring to a boil for five minutes. Take off heat and stir in the vinegar. Allow to cool, then refrigerate until ready to serve. Some people like it cold from the fridge and some like to heat it before using. Your preference.

THE SIMPLE TRUTH BARBECUE BASTING SAUCE

This vinegar-based sauce is used to baste and flavor your barbecue as it cooks. It is used through the entire cooking process up until the Final Touch Sauce (see recipe) is put on the meat about 30 minutes before you take it off the fire. If kept in a good, tight container and refrigerated, it should last for several weeks.

1 ½ cups vinegar
1 cup of the Final Touch Sauce
4 cups water
2 tbl. salt
2 tbl. black pepper

Mix ingredients well and store in tight container.

FINAL TOUCH BARBECUE SAUCE

You would not believe what some people put in their barbecue sauce. In one of my favorite books on barbecue, *Real Barbecue* by Greg Johnson and Vince Staten, one secret recipe calls for—and I am not making this up—cough syrup in the sauce. To me, that is barbecue genius, and I would love to savor those folks' barbecue, but unless you are the type of person who likes chili powder in your ice cream, you really don't need more than a few staple ingredients to make a great—I said *great*—barbecue sauce. This is NOT a table sauce, but is used specifically on your meat to coat it about 30 minutes before taking it off the grill. In your last 30 minutes you might even want to slather this on twice. After you have basted the barbecue with the Simple Truth Basting Sauce it will be good and flavored. However, the Final Touch Barbecue Sauce is to give your barbecue that final wonderful kick of tomato-based flavor.

1 8-oz. can tomato paste
1 16-oz. can tomato sauce
1 cup vinegar
4 tbl. Worchestershire sauce
2 cups water
1 ½ tsp. black pepper
½ cup onion, chopped fine
½ tsp. salt or to taste

Preparation:

Combine all ingredients in sauce pan. Bring to boil and simmer 15 minutes. Keeps well in refrigerator.

DIY BBQ RUB

There are many superb commercial BBQ rubs at your favorite grocery store. But I promise you this do-it-yourself rub will match any of them and flavor your meat deliciously.

Use equal amounts of the following:

granulated garlic
salt
Adolph's Seasoned Tenderizer
black pepper
paprika

Preparation:

In a mixing bowl add equal amounts of all listed ingredients and mix well. Put in air-tight container which will keep the rub fresh for many weeks. Put on chicken, ribs, lamb, you-name-it with a heavy coating. When grilling, allow your meat (or fish) that has been coated to crust over as it cooks over the coals, about 15 minutes on each side before adding any type of marinate.

AUNT NORA'S BUTTERED AND ROASTED PECANS

I'm not sure what it was about pecans, but the extended Graves family adored these elegant nuts and used them in all kinds of recipes. My father was passionate about growing pecan trees and managed to oversee trees in our front and backyards from saplings to prodigious producers of their fine nut meats. I remember vividly my Mom and Dad with great Tupperware containers of pecans, shelling them with a hand-cranked nutcracker, picking out shell remnants from the pecan, and setting aside perfect and sublimely tasty nuts. Mom made fantastic pecan pies with these fresh pecans. She could have won awards at state fairs.

My Aunt Nora, who was the same age as my grandmother, was a dear relative of ours in Arkansas who we loved to visit because she would dote on my brother and me and feed us good things. Her specialty—and the whole Graves family knew it—was roasted pecans that were cooked in butter and salted. My Uncle Richard in particular wouldn't go on a long trip without a dispatch to Aunt Nora to whip him up a batch.

It's a simple recipe but needs love and tenderness and a sharp eye to find perfection. Good luck.

4 cups of whole-piece pecans
½ cup of melted butter
salt to taste

Preparation:

Line baking pan with aluminum foil. Spread layer of pecans evenly in pan. Drizzle butter to cover all of the pecans. Sprinkle liberally with salt. Bake in 350 degree oven for 20 minutes or so, stirring occasionally, until pecans have a nice toasty look to them. Cool for 10 minutes. Enjoy.

FRESH PINEAPPLE AND CURRY POWDER

Tom Graves

In a previous lifetime I worked as a marketing executive for a prestigious Memphis firm. One of the few perks of working the grueling hours there was being invited to dine in the executive dining room. The room was divided into a north side and a south side. The south side, if memory serves me, is where the boss ate, and if you were invited to the south side it meant a full hour of jangled nerves and a stomach full of butterflies. The north side, however, was relaxed and convivial, and we were served wonderful gourmet meals prepared by the late Wilma Madison, an African American woman who was hired almost right out of high school as a chef at Justine's, for years Memphis' toniest, most elegant restaurant. Wilma was already renowned as a soul food cook; Justine's elevated her art into full French cuisine. She was hired to oversee the executive dining room during my tenure at the company. Often I would sneak away from my marketing duties to talk food with Wilma. I still have notes she wrote for me then.

I can't recall exactly when, but Wilma is the one who introduced me to the fantastic flavor fireworks of combining fresh pineapple with a good curry powder. It may not sound appetizing, but I promise your tastebuds will stand up and applaud. These two wonderful flavors work some sort of magic together—the sweet with the spicy—and provide a tantalizing appetizer with any meal.

The curry brand I use is Sharwood's Medium Curry Powder. Heaven!

1 pineapple cut into segments of your preference
Curry powder

Preparation:

Take fresh pineapple and cut into appropriate serving pieces. Sprinkle lightly with curry powder and serve.

A SOUL FOOD CHRISTMAS DINNER

Tom Graves

Menu for Ms. Larthy's Christmas Soul Food Dinner

Turkey
Ham
Dressing
Cranberry sauce slices
Ms. Larthy's Work of Art Macaroni and Cheese
Ms. Larthy's Sunday School Social Potato Salad
Turnip greens
Yams
Coconut cake
Ms. Larthy's Better Than Scratch Banana Pudding
Iced Tea
Ms. Larthy's Special Party Tea
Sliced fresh tomatoes

When Ms. Larthy and I began to layout the master plan for this cookbook, one thing we both agreed would add a special touch for anyone using this book on a regular basis in their cooking lives was a menu with recipes of an appropriate Christmas soul food dinner. What you see in this section is what Ms. Larthy has prepared for her family at Christmas since she was first married. These are the dishes that are her family tradition and her daughters, grandchildren, nieces, nephews, and others would not feel it was a proper Christmas without a table laden with this food.

Because we were wrapping up my final cooking lessons in the summer of 2017 for this book, we decided to finish up our last lesson with a bang and have Ms. Larthy's traditional Christmas meal in July with specially invited guests to celebrate with us. The only thing that might be considered out of place in July as opposed to December 25th is the addition of fresh in-season tomatoes. Reverend Roger Brown, the pastor of Greater White Stone Missionary Baptist Church, where my cooking lessons have taken place, joined us along with his wife and gave the traditional food blessing before we sat down to one of the great meals most of us have ever had. It was the perfect conclusion to a year spent cooking, practicing, tasting, learning, and sharing our lives.

The recipes for the following dishes are located elsewhere in this book: Ms. Larthy's Work of Art Macaroni and Cheese, Ms. Larthy's Sunday School Social Potato Salad, Ms. Larthy's Better Than Scratch Banana Pudding, Iced Tea, and Ms. Larthy's Special Party Tea.

Preparation of the turkey should be your own preference, whether baked traditionally with seasonings such as salt, pepper, granulated garlic, oregano, basil, etc. and stuffing, smoked outdoors over coals, or deep-fried in peanut oil as devised by chef Alex Patout.

The ham for our Christmas Dinner was store-bought Honeybaked Ham, which has become a tradition for many in the past generation since preparing a ham at home is hardly worth the tedious effort and, let's face it, the Honeybaked Ham company does a better job with ham than we can.

The other recipes for the Christmas Soul Food Dinner follow.

CORNBREAD DRESSING

6 cups self-rising corn meal
4 eggs (total)
3 cups whole milk
½ cup vegetable oil
4 cans chicken broth
1 stick margarine
1 box Stove Top Stuffing
1 tsp. ground sage

1 tsp. celery seed
½ cup chopped onion
½ cup of chopped celery

Preparation:

First you must make the cornbread. In a mixing bowl stir together 6 cups of corn meal, 2 eggs, 3 cups of milk, and ½ cup of vegetable oil. Bake in 350 degree oven in a skillet, dutch oven, etc. until cornbread is done.

When cornbread has cooled, crumble cornbread into small pieces. Chop onion and celery into small, fine bits and add to cooking dish with crumbled cornbread. Add chicken broth, melted margarine, seasonings and Stove Top Stuffing, and remaining two eggs. Stir well. Bake at 350 degrees for one hour.

COCONUT PINEAPPLE CAKE

1 box of Pillsbury Pineapple Cake Mix
1 cup water
½ cup vegetable oil
3 eggs

Preparation:

Mix all ingredients. Pour into a 28" round cake pan and bake at 350 degrees for 35 minutes or until done. Allow to cool and add frosting and shredded coconut.

FROSTING FOR COCONUT PINEAPPLE CAKE

3 tbl. Crisco shortening
4 ½ cups of confectioner's sugar
2 cups whole milk (adding more if needed)
Shredded coconut

Preparation:

Mix all ingredients except coconut in mixing bowl. Apply onto cake when it is cooled. Last, sprinkle coconut on top and sides of cake until well-coated.

TURNIP GREENS

6 bunches of turnip greens
1 smoked ham hock or hog jowl
1 tbl. sugar (reduce sugar to ½ tsp. if you don't like it as sweet)
1 tbl. salt
1 tsp. black pepper
¼ tsp. crushed red pepper flakes
1 tbl. greens seasoning
3 tbl. bacon drippings
pepper sauce (on your table to use if you want to "kick it up" a few notches)

Preparation:

Pick through greens and remove all unwanted leaves from bunches. Wash greens in cold water at least six times to remove all dirt, grit, etc. Boil the ham hock or hog jowl at least 30 minutes in water to cover. Add greens to the boiling meat and add another 4 cups of water to make sure and completely cover greens. Add all other ingredients mixing well with greens. Keep on low boil for 1 hour and 45 minutes.

Special Thanks To:

Terica Bobo
Reverend Roger Brown
Allison Graves Buchanan
Jordan Buchanan
Mo Carlson
Tom Carlson
Kay Cunningham
Darrin Devault
Gerald Duff
Emma Sue Graves-Elkins
Merle Graves
Richard Graves
Marcia Hale
Linda Kuczwanski
Lydia Dianne Lay
Nora MacAlexander
Dana Merriweather
Yvonne Mitchell
James Newcomb
Bintou Ndiaye
Georgia Noel
Jasmine Parks
Tim Shirley
Linn Sitler
Susan Steffens

OTHER BOOKS BY TOM GRAVES

Fiction
Pullers
Aesop's Fables with Colin Hay

Nonfiction
Crossroads: The Life and Afterlife of Blues Legend Robert Johnson
Louise Brooks, Frank Zappa, & Other Charmers & Dreamers
Graceland Too Revisited (photography with Darrin Devault)
White Boy: A Memoir
My Afternoon with Louise Brooks

Larthy Washington, born Larthy Rogers in 1937 near Tupelo, Mississippi, was nine years old when she began to cook the midday meal for her farm family. She graduated with a degree in Elementary Education from Mississippi Industrial College in 1959 and taught second grade in Lambert, Mississippi until she met and married Earl Washington and moved with him to Memphis. After having two daughters, Ms. Washington became her church cook for the next 40 years, earning a reputation throughout the Memphis church community as an outstanding cook.

Tom Graves is the owner and publisher of Devault Graves Books. Born in Memphis in 1954 he graduated with a Journalism degree from Memphis State University and an M.F.A. degree in Creative Writing from the University of Memphis. He taught college English and Creative Writing for 25 years. He is the former editor of *Rock & Roll Disc* magazine, the author of eight books including the award-winning *Crossroads: The Life and Afterlife of Blues Legend Robert Johnson*, and was a producer and writer for the Emmy-winning documentary film *Best of Enemies*.

www.ingramcontent.com/pod-product-compliance
Lightning Source LLC
Chambersburg PA
CBHW051548220426
43671CB00021B/2980